TIBET:
Natural Resources and Scenery

By Li Mingsen and Yang Yichou

FOREIGN LANGUAGES PRESS

First Edition 2005
Second Printing 2010

ISBN 978-7-119-03454-6

© Foreign Languages Press, Beijing, China, 2010
Published by Foreign Languages Press
24 Baiwanzhuang Road, Beijing 100037, China
http://www.flp.com.cn
Distributed by China International Book Trading Corporation
35 Chegongzhuang Xilu, Beijing 100044, China
P.O. Box 399, Beijing, China

Printed in the People's Republic of China

CONTENTS

One

GENERAL DESCRIPTION

To many, Tibet is a place full of attractions. It has lofty snow-capped peaks, vast expanses of highland pastures, emerald-green lakes of all sizes and a wide variety of wild creatures that roam the highlands. It is also rich in natural resources. Besides, there is a unique "pureness" about Tibet's natural beauty, and the region's mysteriousness is enhanced by its remoteness, which has long been a great appeal to travelers and explorers all over the world.

Tibet was called "Tubo" by ethnic Chinese during the Tang (618-907) and Song (960-1279) dynasties, and "Wusizang" (the Han language transliteration of "Dbus-Gtsang") during the Yuan (1206-1368) and Ming (1368-1644) dynasties. Although it was also referred to as "Tanggute" and "Tubote" during the Qing dynasty (1644-1911), the name "Xizang" has been consistently used since the reign of Qing Emperor Kangxi (1662-1722).

Now an autonomous region of the People's Republic of China, Tibet lies on the country's southwestern border between 26°50'-36°53' N and 78°25'-99°06' E. It covers an area of more than 1.2 million sq km, accounting for about one eighth of the national territory, and ranking second in size after the Xinjiang Uygur Autonomous Region among China's provinces and autonomous

Location of the Tibet Autonomous Region on the Map of China.

Map of administrative divisions of the Tibet Autonomous Region.

regions. It borders Xinjiang and Qinghai to the north, Sichuan and Yunnan to the east and southeast, and Myanmar, India, Sikkim, Bhutan and Nepal as well as the Kashmir region to the south and west.

Under the jurisdiction of the Tibet Autonomous Region are six prefectures, namely, Shannan (Lhoka), Nyingchi, Ngari, Xigaze (Shigatse), Nagqu and Qamdo, and two cities, namely, Lhasa (prefectural level) and Xigaze (county level), with 71 counties under them. Apart from Lhasa, the capital of the autonomous region, and Xigaze, the region's second largest city, other towns in the region include Qamdo, Zetang, Bayi, Nagqu, Shiquanhe, Gyangze and Zham.

I. The Breath-taking Scenery of the "Roof of the World"

The Qinghai-Tibet Plateau is the youngest, largest and highest plateau in the world; hence it is sometimes called the "Roof of the World" and the "Third Pole of the Earth". It is an ideal tourism destination for lovers of nature and ecological tours.

Tibet forms the main part of the Qinghai-Tibet Plateau. Hence, it is also called the Tibetan Plateau. It is bordered to the north by the Kunlun Mountains that extend hundreds of km, and their branch range, the Tanggula (Dangla) Mountains; its southern border is formed by the youngest, biggest and highest mountain range on earth, the Himalayas; its western border is formed by the steep Karakorum Mountains; and its eastern border by the Hengduan Mountains featuring towering cliffs and deep gorges. Traversing the region from east to west is the Gangdise-Nyainqentanglha Range and its branch

Magnificent and charming landscape of the "Land of Snows."

ranges, with an average altitude exceeding 4,000 m. More than 50 mountains in Tibet stand 7,000 m and more above sea level, ten of which are snow-capped peaks over 8,000 m above sea level. The highest of them all is Mount Qomolangma, renowned not only for its height, but also for its unique scenery. The whole plateau decreases in elevation from northwest to southeast, featuring di-

Mount Qogir, the world's second-highest peak.

verse and complex terrains and kaleidoscopic scenery, with high and meandering mountain ranges, precipitous and deep gorges, glaciers, rocky cliffs, deserts and other types of land forms, and a great variety of rare plants and wild animals belonging to the frigid, temperate, subtropical and tropical zones. One also finds such natural phenomena as altitudinal distribution of the four seasons on the same mountain, and different climates in areas only five km apart.

The sky in Tibet is always blue, and the air exhilarating. The climate is unique, complex and diverse, due to terrain, topography and atmospheric environment. Generally speaking, the temperature is low, due to the high altitude, and can vary considerably in a 24-hour period. The air is thin and the precipitation is on the low side, with distinctively dry and wet seasons as well as plentiful sunshine. The climate differs greatly between the northern and southern parts of Tibet. Under the influence of the warm and wet air currents from the In-

dian Ocean, the valleys in southern Tibet are mild in climate and enjoy ample rainfall, with the average annual temperature standing at eight degrees centigrade, the lowest monthly temperature averaging minus 16 degrees centigrade, the highest exceeding 16 degrees centigrade, and the May-September period being the monsoon season. The climate on the northern Tibet Plateau is typically continental, with the average annual temperature staying below zero centigrade, the frost period lasting as long as half a year and the temperature — even in the warmest month of July — not exceeding 10 degrees centigrade. From June to August, the climate is generally milder. In the

Tibet has many lakes of various sizes, mostly salt-water lakes.

monsoon season it often rains at night. There are strong winds in winter and spring. In terms of climate, the most suitable season to tour Tibet is March to October, with the June-September period being the best.

The mountains and pastures in Tibet are dotted with 1,500 lakes of all sizes and descriptions, which account for about 30 percent of the total area of the lakes in China. There are 787 lakes each exceeding one sq km in area. The best-known of these are Nam Co, Yamzho Yumco, Mapam Yumco and Bangong Co. Tibet is crisscrossed with rivers, including the world-renowned Yarlung Zangbo River and its tributaries the Lhasa River, the Nyangqu River and the Nyang River. Tibet nurtures the Nujiang River (the Salween), important tributaries of the upper streams of the Yangtze and Lancang (the Mekong) rivers, the Sengge Zangbo river (also called the Shiquan river, the trunk of the upper stream of the Indus), the Langqen Zangbo river (also called the Xiangquan or Elephant River, the trunk of the upper stream of the Sutlej), as well as some inland rivers.

Tibet is rich in forest and pastoral resources, with the forest area in the eastern part of the region forming an integral whole with the western Sichuan-

Tibetan wetlands are full of life.

northwestern Yunnan forest area. The region ranks fourth in terms of forested area in China and, being one of the five major grazing grounds in the country, the first in terms of acreage of natural pastures.

II. Diverse Natural Resources

(1) Mineral Resources

The Tibet Autonomous Region is one of the areas with the richest mineral resources in China. There are 94 known varieties of minerals, and the reserves of 47 have been verified, with copper and chrome iron deposits and salt lake resources being the dominant minerals. Copper deposits together with other minerals are scattered on the middle reaches of the Yarlung Zangbo in the eastern and southern parts of Tibet.

Tibet boasts the largest number of salt lakes in the world — 250, comprising a total area of 8,000 sq km. The region is a major producer of salt products in

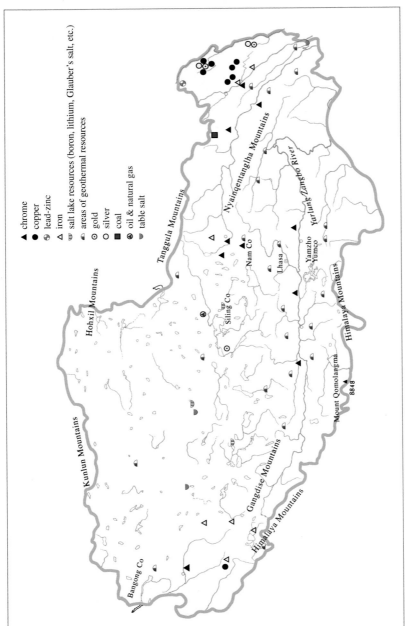

Distribution of major mineral deposits in Tibet.

China, and was the first place in the world to discover and utilize borax from salt lakes.

In addition, oil and natural gas have been discovered in northern Tibet.

(2) Abundant Hydro and Geothermal Energy Resources

Tibet's many rivers and lakes make the region rich in water power. The Yarlung Zangbo, Lancang, Nujiang and other rivers rush down from heights of several thousand m, with big drops, the maximum specific drop amounting to 62 m per m at some sections of the rivers (the lower reaches of the Yarlung Zangbo, for instance). All these rivers have a large volume of water flow, giving the autonomous region a gift of immense hydroelectric potential. The average energy capacity per unit length of the major rivers is 13 to 40 mw per km, and can reach as high as 290 mw per km at some sections along the lower reaches of the Yarlung Zangbo, which is rarely seen elsewhere in the world. Incomplete statistics put the total natural hydroelectric potential throughout the autonomous region at 200,000 mw — about 30 percent of the national total, ranking first nationwide. The generating capacity of the utilizable hydroelectric potential can reach approximately 56,590 mw, with an annual output of 330,000 million kwh, accounting for approximately 17.1 percent of the national total. The average per-capita utilizable hydroelectric potential in Tibet is nearly 60 times the national average.

Located on the Himalayan section of the round-the-globe geothermal band, the Tibetan plateau has the largest reserves of geothermal energy resources in China. A total of 660 spots indicating various hydrothermal activities have been found there. These include hydrothermal explosions, geysers, boiling springs, hot springs, steam zones and sinters. According to preliminary surveys conducted by the Chinese Academy of Sciences on 330 such spots, the total water flow of the hot springs is 20,000 liters per second, with the total amount of thermal energy reaching 660,000 kilocalories per second, or an equivalent of three million tons of standard coal per year; and with a potential power-generating capacity exceeding 800 mw annually. The largest geothermal zone, the Yangbajain geothermal field, has been turned into China's largest geothermal power producer.

(3) Diverse Biological Resources

Tibet has vast expanses of pastures in 17 different types, notably subnival meadows and subnival grasslands that serve as good grazing grounds for highland animal husbandry. Animal species native to the highlands are yaks and Tibetan sheep.

Natural forests are found in the mountainous areas east and south of the Great Canyon of the Yarlung Zangbo. The main types of trees are pine (Pinus wallichiana), highland pine (Pinus densata), Yunnan pine, Huashan pine, Himalayan spruce, Lijiang spruce, western Sichuan spruce, purple-coned spruce, Himalayan fir, sharp-bracted fir, hemlock, large-coned sequoia, Tibetan larch, Tibetan cypress and China lavin. Among them, fir and spruce are predominant, and the reserves of these trees are huge. They are impor-

Giant firs and Huashan pines.

tant building materials because of their straight stems, hardness, fine grain and strength.

The Tibetan Plateau is rich in a wide variety of wild plants and animals. Higher plants number more than 6,800 species, ranking third in China. More than 1,400 of them are of economic value, and many of them are native to the plateau. For instance, of the more than 1,000 medicinal herbs, 300 have special purposes in traditional Tibetan herbal medicine. Among the sugary and starchy plants, juema, popularly known as "ginseng fruit", is highly valued on the dinner table. In addition, there are also fibrous, oil-bearing and aromatic plants, as well as a good variety of wild fruits and fungi, such as pine mushroom, hedgehog hydnum (a kind of fungus that looks like the head of monkey), scaly-tooth mushroom, dried mushroom, black edible fungus and white edible fungus that are nutrient and tasty and contain anti-carcinogens. There are thousands of varieties of garden plants, natural or artificially bred, such as primrose, snow lotus (Saussurea involucrate), azalea, Chinese flowering crab-apple, winter daphne, hydrangea, rough gentian and rose. Wild flowers delight the eyes of visitors to the pastures during the spring and summer seasons.

Tibet boasts 799 species of vertebrates, with birds accounting for 40 percent of the national total, mammals for 32 percent, reptiles for 28 percent, and amphibians for 22 percent of the national total. One hundred and twenty five species of them are on the national list of protected animals, either first or second class, 45 of which are native only to the Qinghai-Tibet plateau, such as the wild yak, Tibetan antelope, wild Tibetan ass and black-necked crane. Eighteen nature reserves have been established to protect the diverse and valuable biological resources and ecological environment of Tibet, with an aggregate area of more than 400,000 sq km, or 33.4 percent of the total area of the region.

(4) Fine-quality Freshwater Resources

The Tibetan plateau is one of the regions in China that have the greatest numbers of rivers and lakes. Some well-known rivers in Asia rise in or pass through Tibet. With total runoff of surface rivers amounting to 448.2 billion cu m, the average surface water per head is seven times the national average. Tibet also has the greatest number of glaciers in the country, totalling 27,400 sq km in area and accounting for 46.7 percent of the national total. Their ice reserves are estimated at 4,757 cu km, approximately equivalent to 75 times the annual flow of the Yellow River into the sea (57.45 billion cu m). In Tibet, where precipitation is small, melted ice from the glaciers is an important source of replenishment for the local rivers and lakes. Thanks to the fact that there is no heavy industry in Tibet, and chemical works are very few, river water is of high quality and little polluted. Except for those rivers in the intraflow region whose water has a relatively high level of mineralization, the level of mineralization in river water is below 100 micrograms per liter. Hence, Tibet has earned a reputation for being "the world's last piece of unspoiled land."

III. The Appearance of Man in the "Land of Snows"

The Quaternary Period is the most recent in geological history, and it is in this period that human beings capable of making tools emerged, from two million to three million years ago.

The uplifting of the Tibetan Plateau was one of the most important geological events on our planet over the last several million years. The extrusion of landmass in the region of present-day Tibet had a decisive impact on the changes in the natural environment of China and Asia as a whole. Therefore, the origin of the formation of the Tibetan plateau and the period of its formation has long been a subject of intense interest to the earth sciences community worldwide.

During the 1970s, a comprehensive scientific study team sent by the Chinese Academy of Sciences to the Qinghai-Tibet plateau discovered in Biru County (4,500 m above sea level) on the Tibetan plateau and Gyirong County (4,100 m above sea level) at the northern foot of the Himalayas fossils of a group of animals, including types of three-toed horses (Hipparion) of the early Pliocene Epoch, including the Tibetan three-toed horse and Gyirong three-toed horse, the Tanggula big-lipped rhinoceros (Chilotherium), Palaeotragus microdon Koken, Heihe low-crest bamboo rat (Brachyrhizomys), extinct elephant, hyena and Gazella gaudry i Schloser. In the sporopollen assemblage of the fossil stratum were found eucalyptus, myrtle, meta-sequoia and mountain longyan (Protea family), which are representative of tropical plants. Also found were snow pine, palm tree, oak and lamb's quarters, which belong to the category of mountainous forest-steppe vegetation in fairly humid subtropical zones. Sites of remnant peak-forest relief similar to those of the limestone areas in present-day south China can be found on various parts of the Tibetan Plateau. All this shows that the Himalayas and the Tibetan plateau at that time were not high, probably no higher than 1,000 m above sea level. The climate then was humid and hot, and the region's geography was tropical woodland and savanna.

The above evidence shows that in the mid-Eocene Epoch, some 30 million years ago, when the last bays of the Tethys, a vast sea, retreated from what is now Tibet, the region did not rise violently all at once, but formed a uniformed planation surface — "initial plateau surface" — in the late Pliocene Epoch, after being subjected to a long period of erosion and deplanation. The basic features of the planation surface bear resemblances to those of the present-day northern Tibet plateau, the only difference being that the altitude of the former was still low, at about 1,000 m above sea level, while the present-day Tibetan plateau, at an altitude over 4,500 m, is the result of the violent upheavals in the earth's crust that caused the extrusion of the landmass over a period of several million years in the late Pliocene Epoch.

Professor Li Jijun and others theorize that the uplifting of the Tibetan plateau in the Quaternary Period showed such clear characteristics as being total, distinctive in stages and accelerated in later stages. Since the late Tertiary Period, because of sharp, wholesale uplifting of the plateau as a result of violent upheavals in the earth's crust, the rivers had no time to cut downwards and the expansive, flat planation surface in vast northern Tibet managed to preserve its original features, maintaining a near-uniform sea level (4,500-5,000 m). Only on the fringes of the plateau did the rushing rivers shape high mountains and deep gorges. The distinctive phases of the plateau's uplifting are manifested in the vertical sections of the river valleys. Generally speaking, the vertical section of a river in Tibet shows three big slope breaks (knick-points). For example, the three knick-points of the Yarlung Zangbo are situated respectively west of Saga County (4,500 m), in Gyaca Gorge (3,500 m) and in the vicinity of Paiqu (2,800 m). The formation of the three knick-points in the vertical sections of river valleys roughly correspond to the three stages of the sharp, violent uplifting of the Tibetan plateau in the late Pliocene, the late Eopleistocene and the late Miopleistocene epochs.

The Tibetan plateau is described as the highest and youngest in the world, because its violent uplifting did not occur until the late Pliocene Epoch of the Tertiary Period. The lofty scenes of the present-day plateau, with an average altitude of 4,500 m, are chiefly the result of the uplifting in the Quaternary Period after the emergence of human beings. Geophysical surveys show that now the Indian Plate is still moving northward approximately at a speed of

50 mm annually, causing the Tibetan plateau to continue its rise at a rate of five to ten mm annually, with the axis part of the Himalayas rising even more rapidly.

What force caused the Tibetan region to become such a colossal plateau in three million years? According to the results of plate tectonics research, the Qinghai-Tibet region sits precisely on a belt of concentrated stress produced by the mutual actions of three rigid plates — the Indian, the Pacific and the Eurasian. On the one hand, the Indian Plate in the south keeps pressing and diving from the south to the north, and on the other, the Eurasian continent in the north presses and dives in the opposite direction, with the rigid eastern landmass constantly pressing and diving in a westward direction, resulting in an extremely complicated structural system in this region. The formation of the Himalayas, Gangdise, Tanggula, Kunlun and Altun mountains, which run roughly from west to east, are probably the result of the push by the older Indian Plate that has made the smaller, younger plates on the southern side of these mountains dive under the Eurasian continent one after another.

After the Indian Subcontinent and the Asian Continent collided and merged in the Neogene period, the seabed expansion of the Indian Ocean did not cease, but continued to drive the Indian Subcontinent to constantly press and dive against the Qinghai-Tibet Plateau, and the blocking by the Tarim land mass to the north made the rock strata at the joining belt of the plates (geofracture) to fold, fracture and rise. During the Quaternary Period, the accelerated expansion of the bed of the Indian Ocean made the Indian plate, the Tarim landmass and the Pacific plate press and dive against the Qinghai-Tibet Plateau with an even greater force, as if wedges were being driven into the base of the plateau from three directions — south, north and east — so that the whole plateau was raised sharply to become the present-day towering "Roof of the World."

THE NORTHERN TIBET PLATEAU—PARADISE OF WILDLIFE

The vast area lying north of the Gangdise-Nyainqentanglha mountain range, which transverses central Tibet, is the famous northern Tibet plateau, also called the Changtang Plateau (in the Tibetan language "Changtang" means "northern highland or empty land"). The plateau extends approximately between 31°-36°40' N and 79°-93° E, and, in terms of administrative divisions, covers the greater part of Nagqu Prefecture and the northern part of Ngari Prefecture of the Tibet Autonomous Region, covering an area close to 700,000 sq km, or approximately 60 percent of the land area of the autonomous region. Its population is only a little over 300,000, accounting for only 12 percent of the total population of Tibet and averaging less than one person per sq km. It is the most sparsely populated area in Tibet, and indeed in the whole of China.

Situated in the hinterland of the Qinghai-Tibet Plateau at an average elevation of 4,000 to 5,000 m, northern Tibet features a severely cold climate, thin air, tundra, grassland and meadows, together with desert and semi-desert.

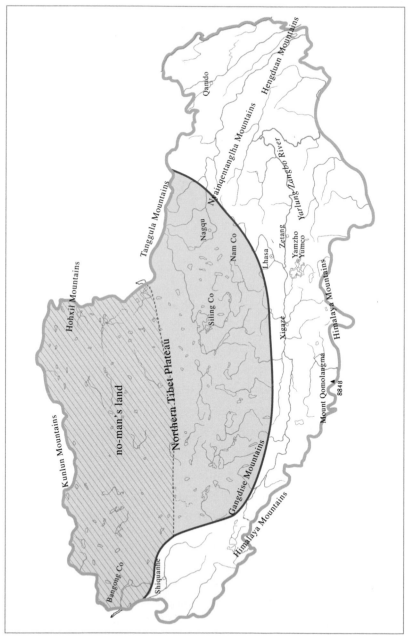

The northern Tibet plateau and its "no-man's land."

Much of this high and cold barren land is an uninhabited wilderness, known as a "no-man's land." The northern Tibet plateau is a vast grazing ground dotted with numerous lakes. Apart from being rich in salt lake resources, it is home to many wild animals.

The tip of the Muztag Glacier (5,400 m above sea level) in the eastern section of the Kunlun Mountains.

Some of Asia's major rivers rise on the Qinghai-Tibet Plateau, which is the largest watershed in the world, and also known as Asia's "water tower." The northern Tibet plateau and the adjacent Hoh Xil area in Qinghai Province constitute the top of this "water tower". For example, the Nujiang River has its origin at the southern foot of the Tanggula Mountains in this area, and the Jinsha River, the upper stream of the Yangtze, and the Lancang River have their origins in the Hoh Xil area at the northern foot of the Tanggula Mountains.

For many centuries, the northern Tibet plateau, especially the uninhabited areas of the "no-man's land" of Changtang, being one of the last few geographical areas not fully explored, has attracted explorers and travelers with the mysteries and exoticism surrounding the land.

Glaciers on the Kunlun Mountains, as viewed from the plateau in the south.

I. Vast Subnival Grasslands

Anyone who steps onto the northern Tibet plateau cannot help but marvel at the grasslands that stretch to the horizon. Especially during the milder summer months, visitors to the Nagqu area will see large herds of cattle and sheep grazing leisurely on the pastures on both sides of the meandering Heihe River under azure skies with patches of white floating clouds, while cooking fire smoke curls upwards from the herdsmen's black tents scattered here and there. Looming far off in the background is a continuous, unbroken range of perpetually snow-capped peaks. Everything seems still in this pastoral landscape. Compared with the grasslands in Inner Mongolia and Xinjiang, the northern Tibetan grassland may appear more open and wilder, but it is

Sheep on a subnival pasture in northern Tibet.

precisely this primitive roughness that adds a unique charm to the appeal of the northern Tibet plateau.

As one of the five major grazing grounds in China, Tibet is rich in grassland resources, with the area of the utilizable natural grasslands exceeding 60 million ha, surpassing Inner Mongolia, Xinjiang, Qinghai and Sichuan to rank first in China in terms of acreage. The utilizable natural grasslands on the northern Tibet plateau cover an area of more than 30 million ha, accounting for more than half of the total in Tibet. As a major pastoral area, animal husbandry occupies a significant position in Tibet's agricultural economy.

The northern Tibet plateau is so vast that the ecological and climatic environ-

ments vary greatly from east to west and from south to north. Generally speaking, the eastern part, with rainfall of more than 400 mm annually, is slightly more humid than the western part, which gets an annual rainfall of less than 400 mm, while the northwestern corner is extremely arid with less than 50 mm of rainfall a year. Corresponding to this, the grasslands there present a variety of types. The three major types are as follows:

(1) Subnival meadows. They are mainly distributed in the Nagqu area in the eastern part of the northern Tibet plateau, consisting mainly of sagebrush, carex, purple Festuca spp, knotweed and other herbaceous plants that are cold-resistant and hydrophilic. The grass generally stands 10 to 50 cm high, with a coverage rate of 80 to 90 percent, so that the meadows look like a green carpet. The quality of the grass is good, making the meadows the best summer and autumn grazing grounds for yaks and Tibetan sheep. Local herdsmen, more often than not, choose to live in clusters here.

(2) Subnival grasslands. These are mostly distributed in the Nyima-Baingoin area in the mid-western part of the northern Tibet plateau, consisting mainly of purple-flower needle grass (Stipa purpurea), S. subsessiliflora, Kunlun needle grass and perennial herbaceous plants that are resistant to cold and drought, such as sand-fixing grass and Tibetan sandy sagebrush, as well as small semi-shrubs. The grass generally stands 10 to 30 cm tall, with a coverage rate of only 20 to 30 percent. Because it is thin and sparse, leaving much of the ground exposed. There are sand dunes swept by the wind. As grazing grounds, such grasslands are inferior to the above-mentioned meadows, but are good enough for Tibetan sheep, which are cold resistant and thermophilic. In the northern part of the plateau, where there is a lack of fresh water, large areas of such pastures cannot be utilized. For example, in the "no-man's land," there are extensive water-deficient pastures. Therefore, only in pockets of

better-watered meadows in the southern part can herdsmen's settlements be found, but far fewer than in the eastern meadows.

(3) Subnival desert steppes. These are mostly found in the northern and north-western parts of the plateau. Because of cold and aridity, they have only a thin cover of Carex moorcroftii, Saussurea and herbaceous plants, and small bushy plants that are resistant to cold and aridity, such as compact ceratoides and spoonmustard, with the coverage rate often below 10 percent and extensive exposed gravels, presenting typical desert or semi-desert scenery. There are almost no inhabitants in these pastures, which are hardly used even for seasonal grazing.

Although on the northern Tibet grassland some pastures are better than others, they are on the whole not as good as those in Inner Mongolia or Xinjiang in

The snow-covered alpine grassland.

Wild yaks.

terms of grass output or quality. The grass on the northern Tibet plateau is not fit for cutting and has a short growing period because of low temperature and snow in winter and spring. The pastures there are suitable for grazing only from May to October, as the grass in winter and spring either withers or needs a period of respite in preparation for the coming grazing season.

There are only a few varieties of domesticated animals that are suited to the harsh natural conditions of the northern Tibet plateau, notably yaks, Tibetan sheep and horses. Yaks and Tibetan sheep, in particular, are widely distributed there and numerous.

Yaks are of the ox family of the artiodactyl order and native to the Qinghai-Tibet plateau. They thrive in cold, humid areas 3,000 m above sea level. Stronger and tougher in build than domestic cattle, an adult male yak usually stands 115-130 cm tall, 130-150 cm in length and 150-190 cm around the chest, and weighs 200-250 kg. It has a pair of thick, curved and sharp horns.

What is most conspicuous about it is its thick coat of long, black hair (some have brown or grey hair, but rarely white). Its short tail, the hair of which almost touches the ground, can be made into whisks to be sold to tourists as souvenirs. White ones are particularly prized. It is very resistant to cold and rarified air. As a result of its adaptability to coldness, high altitude and rarified air over centuries, the yak has developed special physiological features: a broad chest, strong heart and lungs and a high content of haemoglobin — the carrier of oxygen — in the blood, as well as a greater number of red blood cells, so that more oxygen can be absorbed. On account of these special physiological features, yaks can endure the harsh natural conditions of the Qinghai-Tibet plateau, especially the particularly harsh conditions of the northern Tibet plateau.

Yaks have a wide range of uses. They provide the local people with meat, milk, hair, wool and hides. They also serve as pack animals, and pull ploughs. They are as important in the highlands as camels are in deserts. Every part of a yak is useful to Tibetan herdsmen. For example, its hair can be woven into tents, bags and ropes, and its dung is used as fuel and fertilizer. The yak holds an important place in Tibetan mythology and folklore.

The Tibetan sheep is another domesticated animal native to the plateau that has become accustomed to the cold climate, high altitude and rarified air. It thrives in cold and dry conditions, and is equipped physiologically for low atmospheric pressure and low level of oxygen in the air. Compared with sheep living at altitudes below 1,000 m, the Tibetan sheep has a broader chest and is bigger in physique. It has 11 percent more haemoglobin and 28 percent more red blood cells than ordinary sheep. A ram is generally 60-70 cm in height, 83-97 cm around the chest, and weighs 55-100 kg. The wool of the Tibetan sheep is thick and long, giving it good protection against cold. Since the fine wool accounts for about half of the total while the coarse wool accounts for about one third, the wool is of good quality, lustrous and elastic, making it fine material for weaving woolen fabrics and carpets. The famous Gyangze carpets of southern Tibet are made with the wool of the Tibetan sheep as the main material. Nyima, Xainza and Baingoin, and other cold, arid and high-altitude areas in the central-southern part of the northern Tibet plateau are most suitable for raising such sheep and the main producers of sheep for wool to be used in carpet weaving. Called "white silver" by the local people, Tibetan sheep are a major economic resource.

Tibetan sheep are similar to yaks in the scope and altitude of their distribution. Also like yaks, Tibetan sheep are indispensable to the lives of the Tibetan herdsmen, for they can also carry loads, apart from providing meat, milk, wool, fine hair and hides. For example, during June and July each year, caravans of as many as 100 sturdy wethers each carrying a load of 7-10 kg of lake salt in two bags on their backs, can be seen starting their journey from the salt lake areas of the northern Tibet plateau, traveling in a north-south direction across the plateau at a daily rate of 7-10 km, climbing the lofty Gangdise Mountains, crossing the torrential Yarlung Zangbo River and surmounting the towering Himalayas before finally reaching their destination, Nepal, just in time for the harvesting season there. After exchanging salt for grain and other commodities, the Tibetan herdsmen will drive their sheep back along the same route and reach home until the New Year approaches.

II. Lakes Like Stars Studding the Sky

The monotony of the northern Tibet plateau is broken from time to time by lakes, with clear, blue ripples reflecting the surrounding mountains and snow-capped peaks in the brilliant sunshine. Water fowl fly above, or glide over the lake surface.

The numerous lakes, like pearls scattered over a green rug, form yet another spectacle on the plateau. In total, there are some 1,500 lakes in Tibet, big and small, with a combined area of 24,183 sq km, or about 30 percent of the total lake area of the whole of China. The plateau is also the highest lake area in the world, since most lakes there lie at an altitude of 4,000-5,000 m above sea level. The northern Tibet plateau, in particular, boasts no fewer than 1,000 lakes of all sizes, with a combined area of 21,396 sq km, or four-fifths of the total area of all lakes in Tibet, or more than one fourth of the national total lake area.

On the northern Tibetan plateau, in the numerous wide and shallow basins lying roughly in the southern part of the intraflow zone west of the Lhasa-Golmud section of the Qinghai-Tibet Highway and along the belt of depressions at the northern foot of the Gangdise Mountains, replenished continuously by the snowmelt from the nearby mountains, is a cluster of fairly large lakes, such as Nam Co ("Co" in the Tibetan language means "lake"), Siling Co, Zhari Namco, Tangra Yumco, Taro Co and Ngamgla Ringco, ranging between 560 and 1,920 sq km each in area. There are seven lakes in Tibet each exceeding 500 sq km in area. The best-known and also the biggest is Nam Co ("Heavenly Lake"), with an area of 1,920 sq km. Lying at an altitude of 4,718 m, Nam Co is the highest major lake in the world. The next-highest lake in the world is Lake Titicaca, at 3,812 m above sea level, lying on the border of Bolivia and Peru in South America. Apart from Nam Co, there are at least three other big lakes on the northern Tibet plateau, each exceeding 1,000 sq km. in area and lying 4,500 m above sea level (Siling Co, Tangra Yumco and Zhari Namco). In addition, there are 20 medium-sized lakes ranging between 200 and 900 sq km in area and higher than Lake Titicaca on the plateau.

On the vast highland north of Nam Co, lakes are numerous but smaller, because of fewer glaciers and scanty precipitation. There are 207 lakes each exceeding five sq km in size, among which 17 are bigger than 100 sq km. But none reaches 500 sq km. Some of the lakes are "seasonal," due to insufficient water replenishment, so that they are filled with water in summer and dry up or become saline bogs or salt flats in winter.

In short, the numerous lakes of different sizes are a special geographical feature of the northern Tibet plateau. The vast interior zone west of the Qinghai-Tibet Highway, which runs north-south through the plateau, is part of the Central Asian intraflow zone, resembling a big basin. Unlike the conditions in the exterior drainage system in the upper valleys of the two big rivers east of the highway, the Nujiang and the Yarlung Zangbo rivers, all the runoff from the rain and snow in the intraflow zone, instead of spreading beyond its boundaries, flows into numerous inland lakes in the basin. The overwhelming majority of the lakes, especially the larger ones, are tectonic lakes result-

Nam Co, a "heavenly lake."

ing from rift and depression. Therefore, signs of tectonic overprints, such as towering ridges facing each other across the lakes, steep lake banks and manifestations of hot springs, can be seen. Some other lakes run in a direction consistent with that of the tectonic lines of the zones so that several lakes are aligned like a string of beads along the structural grain. Typical examples are the lake groups at the northern foot of the Gangdise Mountains and at the southern foot of the Kunlun Mountains on the northern edge of the plateau.

Besides, impacted by the tendency toward aridity during the most recent geological period, many big lakes have shrunk or broken up into several smaller ones. A typical example is Siling Co (4,530 m in altitude and 1,865 sq km in size), Tibet's second-largest lake, lying not far from Nam Co to the east. The smaller lakes around it — Bangkog Co, Yagedong Co and Ngoin Co — were once linked with present-day Siling Co to form part of the ancient Siling Co, which was far larger than the present-day Siling Co. They were separated

from it as a result of the shrinking of the lake. The dozen or so gravel ridges, ranging from five to over 100 m above the surface of the lake, that can still be seen today around the banks of Siling Co, are the remains of the banks left by the ancient Siling Co as it retreated. They attest to a big drop in the level of the water, indicating that in the late Pleistocene Epoch (approximately 25,000 to 40,000 years ago) Siling Co was probably 250 km in length from east to west, and with an average width of 60 to 70 km and an area exceeding 10,000 sq km — seven times the area of present-day Siling Co. Nam Co also experienced similar shrinkage. The gravel dykes and lakeside terraces that can be seen around the lake were also left behind by the ancient lake, the highest of them being more than 20 m above the present-day surface of the lake.

In addition to the remains of ancient lake dykes, sizable plains and even marshes and salt flats have been formed in most lakeside areas around Siling Co, Nam Co and other big lakes, another result of lake shrinkage.

Many of these lake areas are not only uniquely scenic, but also suitable places for communities to survive by fishing and animal husbandry thanks to their good ecological conditions and rich natural resources. For example, the seats of Baingoin, Nyima, Xainza and Coqen counties and some major towns are mostly located in the areas at the northern foot of the Gangdise Mountains, where there is a cluster of big lakes. For example, Nam Co is bordered by extensive flat pastures and plains, which are lush grazing grounds. The lake also provides some fish resources. When spring comes each year, shoals of fish swim upstream along the tributaries of the lake. Because the lake water is low in temperature and clear, with few plankton, there is only a small variety of fish, as is the case with many other freshwater or brackish lakes on the northern Tibet plateau. The chief fish species are naked carp and Schizopygopsis, loach. These fish have few scales. Mostly omnivorous, they can take in as much nutrition as possible within a short food-taking period so as to store sufficient nutrition to tide over dormancy and hibernation in the winter freezing period. They gain weight in the summer, only to lose it in the winter. Thus, they can hardly increase their size; after several years, such a fish will weigh only about half a kg. Big fish are a rare sight. Moreover, these fish produce nine-tenths fewer eggs than those on the plains. Hence, the low breeding rate and limited fish resources in the lakes.

Some lakes are ideal habitats for many species of birds. For example, some isolated islets in Nam Co are home to groups of brown-headed gulls, bar-headed geese and reddy shel-ducks (called locally "yellow ducks"). They hover over the lake freely, and propagate on the islets undisturbed. Birds' eggs are found everywhere on the islets, which are natural breeding grounds for wild ducks. Such "bird islets" are special scenes on the northern Tibet plateau. They can also be found in Co Ngoin near Siling Co and Angdar Co in the northern "no-man's land."

Wild birds in a pristine environment.

The local people regard many lakes as holy, and pay homage to them. All kinds of myths and legends about them circulate. Nam Co is one of them. Legend has it that the patron of the lake is the kind-hearted daughter of a dragon, who blesses the populace and protects the sheep. Therefore, every Year of the Ram by the Tibetan calendar people converge from all directions to pay homage to the lake, many trekking hundreds of miles on foot. On arrival, they circle the lake clockwise, turning prayer wheels in their hands and reciting scriptures, in the hope of storing up happiness both for this life and for the next. The pilgrims, either on foot or on horseback, stop frequently to kneel down and touch their foreheads to the ground as they go along. The popular belief is that the more circles of the lake one makes, the greater happiness one accumulates. Usually it takes one month to make one circuit of the lake.

Some lakes are also favorite scenic spots. Among them are Yamzho Yumco in southern Tibet, Conggo, Yi'ong and Rawuco in southeast Tibet, and Mapam Yumco in Ngari. Nam Co in northern Tibet has become a major attraction for Chinese and foreign tourists alike.

Visitors to the Nam Township on the lakeside plain of Nam Co will find neat rows of one-story houses and an assemblage of tents, blue, white or black in colour. Red flags flutter over most of the tents. Farther away, on the green pastures herds of cattle and sheep graze quietly, against the backdrop of the snow-capped Nyainqentanglha Mountains to the south.

Those who wish to explore this area further may include in their itinerary an excursion to the Zhaxido Peninsula that juts about three km into the center of the lake from its eastern bank. Apart from the Zhaxi ("Zhaxi" in Tibetan

A redshank.

means "auspicious") Monastery, what attracts visitors is the grotesque ancient karst features on this tiny limestone peninsula, such as pillars of stone, caves, stone arches and stone pillars. The stone pillars that stand like guards on the lakeside terraces on the edge of the peninsula resemble a mushroom or an elephant's trunk or a Buddha's palm.

Wild yaks grazing on the plateau.

Some pillars have round or elongated holes through which one can have a view of the lake.

III. Salt Lakes

Most lakes on the northern Tibet plateau, almost 1,000 in all, are brackish and salt lakes. The southern part of the intraflow region has a bigger portion of brackish lakes, such as Nam Co, Siling Co, Zhari Namco, Tangra Yumco, Angdar Co, and other large lakes that show a mineralization level above 10 g per liter. The number of lakes with a mineralization level exceeding 35 g per liter are fewer, notably Bainkog Co, Cam Co and Chabyer Caka ("Caka" in Tibetan means "salt lake"). Only a small number of lakes are freshwater ones, like Gyaring Co, Urru Co and Co Ngoir. In the more arid northern part, most lakes are salt ones with a high mineralization level (generally ranging be-

A typical Tibetan salt lake.

tween 100 and 200 g per liter, or even exceeding 300 g per liter in some cases), followed in number by brackish lakes, while freshwater ones are rare.

These salt lakes were formed because the medium-sized and small lakes tucked in the heartland of the plateau did not have sufficient replenishments from rain and snow over a long time, and the long years of evaporation made their water level drop continuously, resulting in decreased water flow, while the water was increasingly enriched and salinized, until the lakes dried up. The salt content of quite a few lakes, like Margog Caka and Margai Caka, in the "no-man's land" of northern Changtang, is already super-saturated, so that a large amount of white salt crystals have been deposited on their beds. Margog Caka has already dried up. During the rainless winter season, the white salt crystals at the bottom of the lake glisten in the sun, and look like a giant skating rink. The rainy summer turns it into a seemingly ordinary lake, when a shallow layer of water covers the bed of salt.

However, some salt lakes present a scene different from that of Margog Caka. There is a small salt lake called Cedo Caka not far from and southeast to the seat of the government of the Shuanghu (Twin-lake) Special District. Although its mineralization level, at 280 g per liter, is not as high as that of Margog Caka, at 318 g per liter, what is special about it is a layer of white salt efflorescence, as thick as 20 cm at some points, on its gently sloping banks. Seen from a distance, this white layer may be mistaken for remnant snow, but if one removes the powdery crust, what is revealed is white, translucent grain-shaped or cylinder-shaped salt crystals that glitter in the sun.

Brine-type salt lakes with a mineralization level as high as that of Margog Caka and Cedo Caka are not uncommon on the northern Tibet plateau. Apart from their extraordinary landscape, they are also highly valued for their rich and varied salt resources. The brine has a large concentration of table salt, alkali and Glauber's salt, ripe for commercial exploitation. Many salt compounds were discovered for the first time in China, and boast large reserves, making these lakes inexhaustible natural salt mines. Salt, borax and potassium are the most important of their products.

The northern Tibet plateau's huge reserve of salt is astonishing. Take Margog Caka for an example. With an area of only a little over 70 sq km, it has a sedimentation of salt crystals at least one meter in thickness on its bed. At a rough estimate, its reserve of table salt alone would be enough to supply the three-million population of Tibet for 10,000 years. There are innumerable such lakes, big and small, in northern Tibet. The salt is of fine quality and sells well in Nepal and India. Traditionally salt from northern Tibet was carried by caravans to neighboring countries to exchange for grain. Lake salt is an important special commodity of the northern Tibet plateau and has an immense potential for exploitation.

Northern Tibet is also well known for its production of borax. The region has a record of mining and using borax as early as the sixth century. Today, over 10,000 tons of borax is shipped to different parts of China every year. Most salt lakes in northern Tibet contain borax as the main item. The exact amount of the borax reserves has not yet been verified. Borax, which was first used in medicine, is now widely used in the metallurgical, glass-making and space industries.

The salt lakes are devoid of fish, but are suitable for the growth of artemia, algae and other halophiles. Artemia is good feed for young shrimps, a specialty of Bohai Bay in China, and can remove organic pollutants from the water bodies of salt lakes. Hence, it has a very high economic and ecological value. Algae can be used for the extraction of ?-carotene, glycerine, fatty acids, algae protein, chlorophyll and tetraene oil, and therefore are of high nutritious value. Both artemia and algae from the salt lakes on the northern Tibet plateau promise broad prospects for development.

IV. The Mysterious "No-Man's Land"

The northern part of the intraflow zone on the northern Tibet plateau, a vast zone lying approximately between 32° N and the Kunlun Mountains to the north that divide Tibet from Xinjiang, is what is usually called a "no-man's land," stretching over more than 200,000 sq km and at an average altitude exceeding 5,000 m. The climate there is severely cold, and the air is very thin, with the oxygen content about half that in the low land of eastern China. People going there for the first time usually find it hard to breathe and move about because of the lack of oxygen, and exhibit symptoms of mountain sickness. In the long winter, the temperature can drop to 30 to 40 degrees below zero centigrade. Only few days, in July and August, offer an average temperature higher than 10 degrees centigrade. Even on warmer summer days, the precipitation is mostly in the solid state of snow and hail. The area in the vicinity of latitude 32° N is prone to hailstorms in northern Tibet, with the number of hailstorm days averaging one month a year, and the number of days with winds having a force of 17 m per second or stronger exceeding 200 days a year. The vegetation cover is thin and short. It does not turn green until June sets in, and begins to turn yellow before September begins. Therefore, it is not suitable for grazing. It is a permafrost area, where there

Tundra marshland on the northern Tibet plateau.

are very few surface rivers, and the numerous small lakes are mostly salt ones, so it suffers from an acute shortage of potable water. A combination of all these unfavorable factors has greatly limited the possibility of human habitation and grazing activity there. So, human beings and domestic animals are a rare sight. This expansive wilderness can be mentioned in the same breath with the Taklimakan Desert in Xinjiang, which is referred to as the "sea of death." For centuries, it has remained one of the few geological blanks on the earth not yet fully explored. Thanks to a number of expeditions conducted on and off over the last century, people began to have a better knowledge of the area, which has been variously referred to as a "land forbidden to mankind" and a "land of death," and lifted its veil of mystery. This extremely wild and severely cold area has been found to have many natural features and special landscapes little known to the outside world. Apart from the above-mentioned numerous lakes and rich lake salt resources, it offers special sights that are rarely seen elsewhere in Tibet. For example, the vegetation there is entirely different from that in any other place in the world. It consists mainly of plants belonging to the subnival grassland, with purple flower needle grass, *Stipa subsessiliflora* and *Festuca spp.* as the main plants, supplemented by *Poa spp.*, sandy needle grass and stiff-leaf carex; and of plants belonging to the subnival wilderness, with *Ceratoides compacta* as the most common, supplemented by *Ajama fruticulosa* and *Ephedra spp.* They are short and grow sparsely, with the coverage rate generally below 30 to 40 percent, and which can drop to as low as five percent or even lower. These two plants are the grassland and wilderness vegetation found growing at the highest altitude and most extensively in the world. The exposed ground consists mainly of gravels or semi-shifting sand dunes, similar to the arid wilderness of northwest China.

Some wide and shallow low-lying land and dry riverbeds are often covered by shield-like bodies of ice in diverse sizes. These translucent chunks of ice are a commonly seen periglacial feature in the permanently frozen "no-man's land". They are cone-shaped ice bodies. When the water from surface rivers or spring water flowing from underground is frozen before spring comes, it turns into what are called ice pinnacles in geomorphology. They vary in size, usually forming big oval-shaped ice bodies with a surface of several sq km and more than one m in thickness. They begin to melt gradually in summer, until they disappear altogether. Some individual chunks, even though not completely melted, disintegrate into smaller pieces. The melt water has a fairly low mineralization level, at one to 1.5 g per liter, and is fresh or slightly brackish water potable by human beings and animals. These ice bodies are a highly prized source of drinking water as they serve as natural "solid-state fresh-water reservoirs," which store most river/spring water in the form of ice in winter, and release it in the form of melt water when it turns warmer.

They thus provide drinking water for wild animals, and moisturize the land, bringing the plateau back to life.

In the northern part of the "no-man's land," at the foot of the Kunlun Mountains, there are some horseshoe-shaped extinct volcanoes, flat-topped, square-shaped hills (also called table-shaped hills) formed by lava, lava plateaus and plains. Such volcanic geomorphology is not seen elsewhere in Tibet. These well-preserved volcanic features attest to the violent eruptions accompanying the crust-breaking tectonic movements in the course of the violent uplifting of the plateau in the early Quaternary Period. As evidence of ancient violent tectonic activities on the Qinghai-Tibet Plateau, there are three groups of volcanoes in the "no-man's land": they are, from north to south, the Qiangbaci, Yurba Co and Bamaoqungzong groups of volcanoes. Within the southernmost Bamao-qungzong group one can find a typical volcanic cone, which is an example of proto-volcanic geomorphology. It stands 200 m above the ground, with a funnel-shaped crater and an opening on the southeast side, through which lava once flowed. The volcanic cone is well preserved. On the volcanic plains lying around the volcanic core are many stone pillars and balls, which are the result of basalt erosion. Arrayed in a disorderly

Measuring the temperature of a geothermal spring.

manner, they are in grotesque shapes. Some are just piles of stones, reminiscent of medieval European castles.

Near Bamaoqungzong more than 30 artefacts pertaining to human activity in the Middle or early New Stone Age, 7,500-5,000 years ago have been found. They include scrapers and other stone tools, indicating a culture somewhat earlier than the Yangshao culture of China's central plains, and evidence that the climate of the "no-man's land" in that period was mild enough for human survival. The analysis of the animal and plant fossils and sporopollens of extinct plants in local sediments of the Quaternary Period, including lake facies strata, and isotope radiation C-14 dating also show that the climate in the central-south area of the northern Tibet plateau during the mid-Holocene Epoch was relatively mild. Numerous animals of the forest type, such as giraffes, hyenas, rhinos, three-toed horses and other mammals, roamed the plateau, on which pine, birch, oak and other conifers as well as broadleaf trees grew. That was the period when the human activity on the Tibet plateau was reaching its limits, as the climate turned warmer and the ancients who had originally lived in lower areas began migrating to higher places and to the northern part of the plateau all the way to the Bamaoqungzong area lying approximately at latitude 34° N. The sites of these stone artefacts are close to lakes or springs. Such an environment favorable for human survival experienced a tremendous change approximately 3,000 years ago, when the late Holocene Neo-Ice Age set in. With this, the climate turned colder and drier, many lakes shrank and were salinized, and highland forests gave way on the northern Tibet plateau to herbaceous and small shrubby plants that were thin, short and resistant to drought. The change in the fishing and hunting resources by which the ancients had made a living and in the ecological environment forced them to migrate to lower ground in the south, which was more suitable for habitation.

V. "Masters" of the Plateau

The law of the jungle, that is, the survival of the fittest, is well illustrated in this ecologically harsh "no-man's land." Rare species of wild animals native to the Qinghai-Tibet Plateau, like the Tibetan wild ass, wild yak and Tibetan antelope, as well as the Tibetan gazelle, argali and blue sheep, as well as a limited number of wolves, foxes, lynxes, brown bears and other ferocious animals, are the main wild animals which have adapted to the conditions there. Among the local birds are black-neckeded cranes, bar-headed geese, reddy shelducks, brown-headed gulls and other migratory birds, and such native birds as the Tibetan snowcock and ground jay. Wild rabbits and pikas (rat-rabbits) are to be seen everywhere on the plateau. The latter look like rats but actually are not, and are destroyers of the grassland.

The most attractive rare species on the plateau are the Tibetan wild ass, Tibetan antelope, wild yak and black-necked crane. The first three animals are large or medium-sized herbivores, large in numbers and distributed widely, and can be said to be the "masters" of the northern Tibet plateau. They can be seen galloping on the vast grassland, or spotted in the bushes. Zoologists and photographers alike follow them with intense interest.

The Tibetan wild ass, of the horse family in the perissodactyl order, is similar to a horse in appearance; hence it is also called a wild horse. There are two kinds of wild asses in the world at present, African and Asiatic, both being typical desert and grassland animals. The Asiatic wild ass is subdivided into the Iranian wild ass, Mongolian wild ass and Tibetan wild ass. The latter is mainly scattered on the Qinghai-Tibet Plateau, with the northern Tibet plateau being its main habitat. Tibetan wild asses are good runners, can go without water for several days in succession, and can digest coarse food. These physiological advantages enable them to propagate on the northern Tibet plateau despite the harsh natural conditions there. They tend to stay in groups of from four or five to several dozen or even close to a hundred. They are also "disciplined," with each group having a leader; wherever the leader goes, the rest of the group follow in a single file. The wild asses are capable of running at 45 kph, and over short distances they can exceed 60 kph. There are large numbers of them in northern Tibet, and Nyima County alone boasts 400,000 to 500,000.

Tibetan wild asses in "no-man's land."

The wild yak, of the ox family, artiodactyl order, is a black-haired bulky animal. The wild yak is larger in build than the domesticated yak, and has a pair of thick, sharp-tipped horns. It is fierce and tough by nature, has a very keen sense of smell and looks very ferocious with its tail turned upward when enraged. It is accustomed to living in frigid areas 4,000 m above sea level. Its thick coat of body hair and its thicker layer of fat protect it from cold even when lying in snow. As far back as the early Quaternary Period, when glaciers covered the globe and the climate was cold everywhere, the ancestors of wild yaks roamed north China, Inner Mongolia and northern Eurasia. Later, as the global climate turned warmer, their descendents were limited to the Qinghai-Tibet Plateau and the adjoining Kashmir Plateau. Like the Tibetan wild ass, the wild yak is a first-class nationally protected animal. The present number of wild yaks in northern Tibet is less than 10,000, fewer than that of the Tibetan wild ass.

Wild yaks tend to move in groups. They can climb slopes and ridges easily on the account of their stamina and strong limbs, so hunters generally find it hard to overtake them. They roam the highland grassland or desert grassland 4,000 m to 5,000 m above sea level all year round. Having a ruminant stomach, they can digest needle grass, carex, sagebrush and other coarse herbaceous plants found in the harsh environment of the northern Tibet plateau.

The ancestors of the Tibetan ethnic group gradually domesticated wild yaks, and raised them for meat, milk and hides, as well as for carrying loads and pulling plows. Crossbreeding domestic and wild yaks produces a species superior to the common domestic yak in build and growth.

The Tibetan antelope, which is common on the northern Tibet plateau, is also of the artiodactyls order, but of the Tibetan antelope genus. Slightly smaller than a Tibetan goat in build, a male Tibetan antelope has a pair of long, sharp-tipped and elegant horns (the female is hornless). Each horn measures nearly half a meter in length. Tibetan antelope horn does not have the same special antipyretic effect as the horn of the saiga antelope of Central

A male Tibetan antelope.

Migrating Tibetan antelopes.

Asia, with which the Tibetan antelope is akin, but it still receives considerable attention in traditional Tibetan medicine, for it has a certain sedative and antipyretic effect, and is often used as a substitute for saiga antelope horn. The Tibetan antelope uses its horns as weapons not only for self-defence, but also against rival male antelopes during the mating season. Folk stories have it that every November, when female antelopes are in heat, thousands of Tibetan antelopes gather somewhere in the "no-man's land", and a life-or-death battle erupts among the male ones in fierce rivalry for mating partners. The pregnant female antelopes give birth half a year later, and have one or two offspring at a time. Expectant mothers begin an exodus in groups at the turn of spring and autumn to converge on a mysterious spot in the northern part of "no-man's land" for collective delivery there. Observations that have been conducted in recent years reveal that the Taiyang (Sun) Lake-Zonag Co area in the heartland of Hoh Xil in neighboring Qinghai Province is one of the important "collective delivery rooms." The pregnant antelopes arrive at the Taiyang Lake-Zonag Co area around July when the sunshine is at its fullest and the grass at its most luxuriant. An antelope would continue its journey to the destination even if it gave an early birth on its way. The newborn is able to stand up immediately after the birth, and such a calf would follow its mother antelope to the destination. After delivering and resting for a few days, the female antelopes, followed by their calves, start their return journey in groups to reach in the "no-man's land" before the severest part of winter sets in. They travel to and fro along the same route over hundreds of km, in a manner similar to the birds' seasonal migrations along a route that has never changed over centuries, a phenomenon that has puzzled biologists.

The Tibetan antelope is timid by nature, and swift and agile; it will flee at the slightest rustle of leaves in the wind. A closer look at it reveals that it has a broad nose, with the two sides of the nasal cavity bulging like round air bags, so that it can take in more oxygen and run swiftly despite the thin air to escape from predatory wolves. Its maximum speed can exceed 60 kph. With plants of the grass family and the sedge family as its main food, it has an even greater tolerance for coarse grass than the Mongolian gazelle. It is a rare animal native to the plateau.

Migrating Tibetan antelopes.

The Tibetan antelope's hair is very thick, soft and fine, and quite uniform in length, enough to protect it from the severe cold. A Tibetan antelope yields about 150 g of cashmere wool a year. The expensive "shahtoosh" shawl in fashion in India and Pakistan and woven with Tibetan antelope cashmere wool, is a prized item of a bridal dowry. One such shawl, measuring 2 m by 1.5 m and weighing 100 g, can fetch 40,000 U.S. dollars on the European and American markets. A "shahtoosh" shawl is so fine that it can be rolled up and slipped through a finger ring, so it is also called a "ring shawl."

The Tibetan antelope is generally distributed in the highland and desert grassland 4,000 to 5,500 m above sea level. At present, there are approximately 100,000 Tibetan antelopes in existence, with the majority (about 70,000) living on the northern Tibet plateau.

The "no-man's land" is the main habitat of the Tibetan wild ass, wild yak and antelope. In order to protect the fragile ecological system of the highland grasslands and the rare animals there, the state-level Changtang Nature Reserve was established there in 1993, encompassing the Shuanghu Special Area and the northern parts of Nyima and Gerze counties. With a total area of 298,000 sq km, it is the largest of its kind in Tibet and one of the world's few reserves specially set up for the purpose of protecting high-altitude wild life.

Adjacent to the Changtang Nature Reserve is the Xainza Nature Reserve. Some 40,000 sq km in area, it was set up in the great lakes area in the southern part of the northern Tibet plateau for the purpose of protecting the black-necked crane, which is regarded by the ethnic Tibetans as an auspicious bird. It is native to China, and a valuable and rare species as the only one of the 15 crane species worldwide that lives on a plateau. It is on the national list of first-class protected species, as well as being on the "red data book" of animals on the brink of extinction.

Black-necked cranes.

The name "black-necked crane" is derived from the black ruff around the bird's neck, which sets it off conspicuously from other varieties of cranes. It is accustomed to living on highland lakes, marshland and lakeside bushes, with small fish, insects and aquatic plants as its main food. A migratory bird, it spends the winter on warmer river beaches along the middle reaches of the Yarlung Zangbo River at an altitude of 3,500 m in southern Tibet, or farther south on the Yunnan-Guizhou Plateau. Every March the black-necked cranes swarm back to the lakes and marshland around Xainza. The Xainza Nature Reserve, located at an altitude of 4,600 m to 4,900 m, is the largest and highest among the seven black-necked crane reserves in China. Surveys show that about 4,000 black-necked cranes, or about 70 percent of the world's total, spend the winter in Tibet.

Apart from the rare animals described above, there are other animals unique to the northern Tibet plateau. One example is pika. The pika looks like a rat, but has a very short tail that is almost invisible under its body hair. It belongs to the same Lagomorpha order as the common rabbit, but is not of the same family, though it is commonly called a rat-rabbit as it has similar teeth and habits to the common rabbit. Pikas live on pastures around 5,000 m above sea level, on river and lake beaches and slopes strewn with gravel. They are scattered all over the Qinghai-Tibet Plateau and its neighboring areas. There is a wide variety of them, the most common being the black-lipped pika. The pika has a coat of short, thick hair, with a thick layer of under-wool to keep the cold out. What is special about these small creatures is the fact that small birds, notably Hume's ground jay and snow finches, can be seen flying into and out of their holes. This phenomenon of rabbits and birds sharing the same holes is referred to in some ancient Chinese books. For example, the *Book of History*, *Records of the Historian*, *Book of Mountains and Seas* and *Er Ya* (a Han Dynasty book containing commentaries on the classics) all have brief descriptions of this phenomenon, but without giving explanations. However, contemporary scholars speculate that Hume's ground jay and snow finch use pika holes to ward off the scorching sun, snowstorm and hailstorm because of the scarcity of trees on the plateau. At the same time, the presence of small birds in pika colonies may be useful to the pikas as a warning device in case of the approach of their enemies — hawks and falcons. Thus, this may serve as an example of mutual utilization in the natural world.

In short, the northern Tibet plateau is a kingdom of wild animals. The rare animals native to the plateau and many other highland animals are a bank of valuable biological resources and blastogenesis, and one of the major natural and historical heritages of the world.

Three

NGARI — THE ROOF OF THE PLATEAU

Located in the western part of Tibet, Ngari Prefecture covers an area of more than 310,000 sq km. It is separated from Nepal and India by the Himalayas to the south, and is contiguous to India and the Kashmir region in the west, with a boundary line of 116 km and more than 60 mountain passes leading to other countries. It is separated from Xinjiang by the Kunlun Mountains in the north, and is contiguous to Nagqu and Xigaze Prefectures in the east. Under its jurisdiction are seven counties: Gerze, Coqe and Ge'gyai counties are pastoral, while Gar, Burang, Zanda and Rutog counties are semi-agricultural and semi-pastoral. It has a population of some 60,000, averaging 0.23 persons per sq km. The town of Shiquanhe is the seat of the prefectural government, which is 1,586 km from Lhasa and 1,085 km from Yecheng in Xinjiang.

Ngari has an average altitude exceeding 4,500 m above sea level, hence it is sometimes called the "roof of the world's roof." Four rivers — the Sengqe Zangbo, Konqi Zangbo, Langqen Zangbo and Bamqog Zangbo — named after the lion, peacock, elephant and horse, respectively — have their sources here, and flow on to become the Indus, Ganges, Sutlej and Yarlung Zangbo, respectively.

Ngari once played an important role in east-west economic and cultural exchanges as the Ji Bin (the ancient name of Kashmir) road — the Silk Road linking China with Western, Central and South Asia — passed through this area. Xuan Zang (596-664), a venerable monk of the Tang Dynasty, refers to this area in his *Records of Western Regions of Great Tang*. It was also the

Heishui Lake, Coqen County.

birthplace of the brilliant Shangshung Civilisation. During the Tang (618-907) and Song (960-1279) dynasties, the area was referred to as "Greater and Lesser Yangtong", which is now translated as "Shangshung". During the Yuan Dynasty (1206-1368), it was called "Na-li-suo", and during the Ming Dynasty (1368-1644), "E-li-se", all being historical transliterations of the Tibetan name (Mngav-ris). In the Tibetan-language historical records, Ngari was thought to embrace three regions, hence the traditional appellation, "Three Regions of Ngari." The "three regions" once embraced part of Kashmir.

Ngari's spectacular landscape features snow-capped peaks, glaciers, high-altitude grasslands, deserts, rivers, lakes, farmland, pastures, forests, and an abundance of wildlife. The Guge Kingdom ruins at Zanda, Toling Monastery, the Donggar murals and the Rutog rock paintings are all reminders of the ancient civilisation that once flourished on the plateau. Mount Kangrinboqe, the main peak of the Gangdise Mountains, which is revered as a "holy mountain," and Mapam Yumco, a "holy lake," have a special place in the history of Asian religions. Story-telling to musical accompaniment in Zanda, "xiebaxiema", which is a form of male-female voice duet in Rutog, and story-telling about the legendary King Gesar in Gyegai all have a strong local flavor. Being a place that once nurtured the Tibetan Bon religion and culture, and the Shangshung Civilisation, this is where a traveler begins his or her search for ancient Tibetan civilisation.

A trip to Ngari is a must for those who wish to have a better knowledge of the ancient history and culture of Tibet. Some even go as far as to say that a person cannot claim to have been to Tibet without going to Ngari.

I. The King of the Holy Mountains — Gangdise and Mount Kangrinboqe

The Gangdise-Nyainqentanglha Range, which traverses the central part of the Tibet plateau in an east-west direction, starts at the Sengge Zangbo (Shiquan River) in the west, and curves eastward for 1,600 km to end at the Baxoila Ridge. The range is 80 km from south to north, with an average altitude of 5,800-6,000 m. The two ends of the mountain system are high, while its central part is slightly lower. Its southern flank is steep, with a relative fall of height of about 2,000 m, while its northern flank decreases in elevation more gently, with a fall of only 1,000 m.

Although there are only a few peaks higher than 6,500 m above sea level — Mount Kangrinboqe (6,656 m above sea level), the main peak of the Gangdise Mountains, Mount Lopu (7,095 m above sea level), and Mount Nyainqentanglha (7,162 m above sea level), the main peak of the Nyainqentanglha Mountains — as far as the mountain system as a whole is concerned, the terrain exceeding 5,500 m above sea level is broader, thicker and more complete than the Himalayas and can be described as a giant mountain system with a relative concentration of extremely high mountains.

The Gangdise-Nyainqentanglha Range is an important geographical boundary. Its main body is the divide of the intraflow river system and the exorheic river system on the plateau, with those on its southern flank being exorheic rivers, such as the Sengge Zangbo, which is the upstream of the Indus, and Yarlung Zangbo, while the rivers on its northern flank are much smaller in their scale of development, and most of them empty into inland lakes on the northern Tibet plateau.

Much of the eastern section of the Nyainqentanglha Mountains is covered by snow, and is a major source of the present-day glaciers on the Tibet plateau. The longest maritime valley glacier in China is located here. The glaciers in the Gangdise Mountains to the west are not so well developed. For example, the glacier on Mount Kangrinboqe is only 4,000 m long.

The name "Gangdise Shan" is a mixture of Tibetan, Sanskrit and Chinese words. "Gang" in Tibetan means "snow", "dise" in Sanskrit also means "snow", and "shan" in Chinese means "mountain". The Gangdise ranges are called the "king of holy mountains", and occupies an exalted place in the hearts of Buddhists. Its main peak, Mount Kangrinboqe, is a leading place for Buddhist pilgrimage, and every year, especially in a Year of the Horse in the Tibetan calendar, thousands of pilgrims pay homage to it.

In terms of height, the main peak of the Gangdise Mountains should be Mount Lopu, with a height of 7,095 m, located in Zhongba County. Yet, many religious and historical books choose to regard Mount Kangrinboqe as the main peak, probably because of its irreplaceable position in the Tibetan cultural tradition. "Nyainqentanglha" in Tibetan means "second only to Tanggula," which is also a well-known "holy mountain" in Tibet. The 7,162-meter-high

Mount Nyainqentanglha stands out among the other peaks for its majestic scenery. It is one of the nine indigenous gods of mountains, that is, the Nine Creators of the world, in Tibetan mythology, and is held in esteem by the herdsmen of northern Tibet as a guardian-god of wealth and a god in charge of hailstorms.

Among all the "holy mountains" on the Tibetan plateau, Mount Kangrinboqe in Burang County commands the highest esteem. With its special scenery and its sacred position in Buddhism, it attracts numerous pilgrims and tourists every year. Within an area of 200 sq km around it, there are ten peaks above 6,000 m above sea level and a large number of glaciers, making the area a world-renowned place for mountaineering.

Facing Mount Kangrinboqe, 100 km to the north, is the7,694-m-high Mount Neimona'nyi. Also within Burang County, it is one of the highest peaks in

Mount Kangrinboqe, a "sacred mountain."

Mount Neimona'nyi, on the southern bank of the Mapam Yumco.

the Himalayas, called the "mount of the holy mother" or the "peak of the goddess" by the local people.

The most famous holy mountain in the history of Asian religions, Mount Kangrinboqe is in the shape of a pyramid with a round crown. With its top covered by snow all the year round, glittering in the sun, it towers above a multitude of mountains, overwhelming viewers with its grandeur. However, its top is frequently shrouded in clouds, and it seldom reveals its true features, so there is a mysterious touch about it. At the waist of the mountain is a sizeable terrace in pale red, the edge of which has been seriously eroded by ice and snow, making it jagged, while on the surface of the terrace is a sort of sunken trough. The whole mountain looks like an ancient castle in a shape of a pyramid, imposing and solemn.

Mount Kangrinboqe is formed of arenaceous rock of the late Tertiary Period, with sheer cliffs on all sides. Its snowline is at approximately 6,000 m above sea level, and the area of ice and snow amounts to 2.36 sq km. On its northeast slope is the biggest glacier in Ngari — a typical cirque (bowl-shaped mountain basin) valley glacier, about 2.4 km long, 3.06 sq km in area and with a 5,300-m tip. Another cirque valley glacier on the northern slope is about 1.5 km in length, 0.63 sq km in area, and with a 5,350-m tip. Due to differential dissipation, several small isolated ice pinnacles, about five m tall, stand below the glacier's tongue. The western slope is so steep that although frequent avalanches fall to the bottom of the ancient cirque, no glacier could be formed because of the low altitude of the bottom of the cirque, except for a few avalanche cones. There are five glaciers on Mount Kangrinboqe, with a total area of 6.77 sq km.

Ngari's four major rivers rise near Mount Kangrinboqe, and are named after the four spring wells at their sources, whose heads are said to be shaped like a lion, a horse, an elephant and a peacock, respectively. Hence, the Sengge Zangbo (Shiquan River, upstream of the Indus), Damqog Zambo (Maquan River, source of the Yarlung Zangbo which is called the Brahmaputra after leaving China), Langqen Zamgbo (Xiangquan River, upstream of the Sutlej) and the Konqi River (Peacock River, upstream of the Ganges). These four animals are believed to be deities, and hence Mount Kangrinboqe is regarded as a "holy mountain." In the eyes of the Buddhists there is a sacred connection between the four rivers and Mount Kangrinboqe, which is regarded as the source of all rivers.

II. The Holy Lake and the Ghost Lake

The holy lake, Mapam Yumco, and the ghost lake, Lha'angco, are twin lakes located within Burang County in southeast Ngari, between the Gangdise

Mountains and the western section of the Himalayas.

Mapam Yumco covers an area of 412 sq km, and is 4,587 m above sea level and 77 m at its deepest. To its west is Lha'angco, with an area of 268.5 sq km and being 4,572 m above sea level. The two lakes are replenished by snow-melt from the northern slope of Mount Neimona'nyi in the western section of the Himalayas to the south, making them a freshwater lake and brackish freshwater lake respectively.

The two lakes are flanked by mountains both in the north and south. The top of Mount Neimona'nyi, on the southern flank, at an altitude of 7,694 m, is covered by snow where a series of present-day valley and hanging valley glaciers have formed, with the tips being 5,500 m in altitude. In addition, former mountain glaciation was quite developed, with former glaciers having reached the lakeside, so that a series of morain hills still remain. The Gangdise Mountains on the northern flank have an elevation over 5,500 m, with a few standing 6,000 m or more above sea level. There is an upgrowth of former and present-day glaciers there, with former cirques ranging between 5,200 m and 5,500 m in elevation. The ridges on the east and west sides of the lake basin are low and decrease gently in elevation, and the plains there are wide. The interlacustrine area is linked by waterways near Qiwugongba. According to the report of the Swedish explorer Sven Hedin, in a year of heavy rainfall, a portion of water from Mapam Yumco could flow into Lha'angco. In the summer of 1976, an expedition from the Chinese Academy of Sciences did see a small waterway through which water flowed from Mapam Yumco into Lha'angco. In recent years, because of a drop in the water level of Mapam Yumco and reduced flow of the waterway, the river course has become narrower. Moreover, the central and southern parts of the interlacustrine area are separated by gently sloping hills. As a result of all this, the two lakes are tending toward detachment. A number of stone implements typical of the Mesolithic period have been discovered on the eastern and southeast shores of Mapam Yumco, for example near Hor, especially on terraces 30 m above the water level. This shows that the place was inhabited in remote antiquity.

One of the freshwater lakes with the highest altitude in the world, Mapam Yumco is one of the three holy lakes in Tibet. It is situated more than 200 km from the town of Shiquanhe and about 20 km southeast of Mount Kangrinboqe. It is wide in the north and narrow in the south. Its depth makes the water appear as translucent as a sapphire.

In the Tibetan language, "mapam" means "unconquerable" and "yumco" means "a lake of sapphire". Legend has it that the goddess Wuma, the wife of the god Siva, used to bathe in this lake. The venerable monk Xuan Zang of the Tang Dynasty described the lake as "a fairyland in the west" in his *Records of Western Regions of Great Tang*. In the 11th century, after Buddhism prevailed over the native Tibetan Bon religion, the Buddhists renamed the lake, which had previously been called "Machuico", Mapam Yumco, meaning "unconquerable lake," to signify the victory of Buddhism. Ever since then, Mapam Yumco has been regarded as sweet dew bestowed by the Buddha on mankind with which to cleanse the human soul of the "five evils" — greed, temperament, infatuation, laziness and jealousy — and even more effectively clean the human body of filth so as to make people healthier and longer-lived. Buddhists believe that to make circuits of the lake and bathe in its water can wash away one's wild desires, worries and sins, that the water from the lake is good for one's health, and that making circuits of the lake while praying on a pilgrimage leads to boundless blessings. Many temples were built around the lake, and eight of them now remain. One circuit of the lake covers about 80 km. According to the legend, the lake has four (imaginary) bathing gates on its four sides: the Lotus Bathing Gate on the east, the Fragrant and Sweet Bathing Gate on the south, the Filth-Removing Bathing Gate on the west and the Faith Bathing Gate on the north. The pilgrims are supposed to stop and wash themselves ritualistically at each gate as they walk around the lake in the hope of washing away their sins. Another legend has it that the God of Wealth lives in a palace on the bed of the lake. Anyone who is predestined to get rich will trigger off a flow of wealth into the family if he or she chances on a small fish, a stone or a feather from a gull while making a circuit of the lake. Some pilgrims can be seen tossing gold and silver ornaments into the lake in a show of sincere reverence while chanting prayers. The lake attracts pilgrims and tourists all year round.

The pure ecological environment of Mapam Yumco attracts large flocks of swans to roost there in summer. The swans add grace to the charm of the lake's scenery. The fish in the lake are said to be good for treating infertility, dystocia, dropsy and other illnesses. Laboratory tests show that the water from the lake contains a large amount of trace elements and minerals good for people's health.

The ghost lake, Lha'angco, is much inferior to Mapam Yumco, only three km away, in the quality of its water. Its mineralization level is slightly higher than in Mapam Yumco. The waves are high, and there is little waterweed for fish to feed on. Tibetan Buddhists believe that when a person dies his or her soul first goes to Lha'angco, hence the name "ghost lake".

For centuries, the Mapam Yumco-Lha'angco area, with the two mountains — Kangrinboqe and Neimona'nyi — has been held in esteem as the land of "sacred mountains and holy lakes." The area, in Burang County, is the best-known tourist attraction in the Ngari area. Mount Neimona'nyi, in particular, has always been a focus of interest for mountaineers. A Sino-Japanese expedition became the first team to reach the summit, May 26-28, 1985. Mount

Kangrinboqe, on the other hand, has remained unconquered for a host of reasons.

III. The Earth Forest and the Guge Kingdom Ruins

Near the county seat of Zanda, located between the Gangdise Mountains and the Himalayas, in the Elephant River Valley, lies the impressive "Earth Forest" of Zanda. It is a unique area of gullies as a result of long-time erosion and cutting, by the torrents of big rivers, of the immensely thick sediment layer in the lake basins of large ancient lakes. It covers the several hundred sq km area of whole of Zanda County. Of irregular heights and in diverse shapes, the earthy "forests" look like a fairyland under the hallucinating sunlight and shadows of the highland. Against the background of high and level ridges, earthy "forests" are aligned like arhats or rows upon rows of castles, resembling the scenes of the Colorado Grand Canyons. Especially during the sunrise and sunset, the sunlight casts a magnificent color on the mountain folds. The most beautiful of all is the "earth forest" by the side of the Sengge Zangbo (Shiquan River), near the county seat. The river-side "earth forest" and its abandoned Buddhist pagodas have a mysterious and solemn touch in the deepening dusk. There are several caves with evidence of ancient human habitation, and extensively distributed rock inscriptions. Some scholars think that this is the location of the capital of the ancient Shangshung Kingdom in Bon legends, Qunglung'oika.

The ruins of the ancient Guge Kingdom were included in the first list of key cultural relics for state protection. The ruins of the kingdom's imposing fortified palace are located on a 300-odd-m-high loess hill by the Langqen Zangbo (Xiangquan River), within the Zarang District of Zanda County, 18 km from the county seat. The river has its source in Mapam Yumco, and flows in a northwest direction. Murals, sculptures and wood carvings found in this area display the so-called "Guge art," which was influenced by Buddhist art from India and Nepal while carrying forward the traditional artistic style of the ancient Tubo kingdom.

There are close to 100 caves at a certain place on both banks of the Konqi (Peacock) River. According to legend, they were hollowed out by Kyteh Nyimai Kum when he first came to Ngari, and were where he proclaimed himself king. This was the center of rule for the Ngari area before the Guge palace-castle was built.

Fifteen miles to the south, also on the Konqi River, lies Korqag. Picturesque and pleasant in climate, it is on a trading route leading from Tibet to Nepal. It

Ruins of the Guge kingdom in Zanda County.

is known far and wide for the shrine of Manjusri, a Boddhisattva, in the Korqag Monastery.

IV. Bangong Co and Maindong Co

These lakes are located in valleys between the Karakorum Mountains and Alongganlei Mountains. The twin lakes are very similar in terms of their formation, evolution and features.

Bangong Co lies north of the county seat of Rutog. "Bangong" is translated from Hindi, and means "a meadow". The Tibetan name for it is Como Nganglharingbo Co, meaning "lake of long-necked cranes".

The lake basin of Bangong Co is in the shape of a trough valley. Its body of water is in two parts, linked by small rivers. The eastern section and part of the western sections are within the boundaries of China. Its water surface is 4,241 m above sea level, and it is on average two km to five km wide. The lake basin at the easternmost tip exceeds 10 km at the widest and 41.3 m at the deepest, with small islands. Bangong Co varies in depth. Generally speaking, it is deep where it is wide, and vice versa. At the same time, the water near the northern bank is deeper than that near the southern bank, and the western part is deeper than the eastern part. The water in the eastern part, within China, is relatively fresh and drinkable, because Maga Zangbo, Domar Qu and other fairly big tributaries flow into it, while the water in the western part gradually becomes salty, because the tributaries emptying into the western section provide relatively small replenishment.

Maindong Co lies south of the western section of Bangong Co, and it is a narrow, long inland saline lake at an altitude of 4,300 m and covering an area of 58 sq km. It was once linked with Bangong Co, when the two belonged to the same lake basin system. Later, the two lakes were separated because the trough valley was blocked (west of Rutog County), as a result of the climate turning drier and the water level dropping. The existing linkage is still in the shape of a trough valley, in which there are extensive lake facies accumulation terraces and several small remnant lakes.

The basins of the two lakes are tucked among steep mountains, but due to the arid climate, the former and existing mountain glaciers are not on a big scale, with hanging glaciers as the main form of the existing glaciers, supplemented by a small number of valley glaciers. The ancient cirques to be found around Kana are 5,000-5,300 m in altitude, and their ice-laid drift is unable to reach the lakeside, with the lower limit at 4,400-4,500 m. Most local rivers flowing

Tibetans fishing in the beautiful Bangong Co.

into the lakes are short, with a big specific drop, and there are developed torrential fans at the mouths of the gullies. At bigger gully mouths two-tier torrential fans are commonly seen, with the new fan, which is smaller in scale, covering the old fan, which is larger in scale and can extend to the lakeside and silt up the lakes. At the mouths of the rivers flowing into the lakes are large, developed deltas, with the part above the water clearly visible, as is the case with the Domar Qu Delta and the delta near Kana. These deltas consist mainly of sandy soil on which ground plants grow well. There are extensive lakeside plains in Rutog County, which are an important agricultural and animal husbandry base for Ngari Prefecture.

The portion of Bangong Co within China has clear and sweetish water. It abounds in *Schizothoracin*, a fish of the carp family. The lakeside vegetation is thin and sparse. In the center of the lake is a small islet, 300 m long and 200 m wide, which is the habitat of bar-headed geese, brown-headed gulls, black-necked cranes and 20 other varieties of birds. The birds present a spectacular view when they take to the skies and hover over the lake en masse — they block the sun and their chirping can be heard miles away. The islet is the highest bird nesting place in the world.

If one travels along the Xinjiang-Tibet Highway for 117 km in a northward direction from the Shiquan River in Gar County, one reaches the Rutog County town, the westernmost border town in Tibet. At an altitude of 4,314 m, the county has a population of less than 10,000 people scattered over an area of 75,400 sq km, averaging less than one person per ten sq km. Rutog is a subnival area with animal husbandry as the dominant economic sector. *Qingke* barley, potatoes and a small variety of other cold-resistant crops can be grown in pockets of lower land. There is only some 500 ha of farmland in the county.

V. "Soft Gold"—Cashmere Wool

Although Ngari is a subnival and arid area lacking in thermal resources and with an annual precipitation of less than 200 mm, it has abundant sunshine — 71-76 percent of the year, and with the total number of sunshine hours exceeding 3,150 hours per year. The town of Shiquanhe has 8,200MJ per sq m of solar radiation, the highest amount in the whole of China. Under such climatic conditions, the natural grasslands are mainly desert grasslands, with the remainder being subnival grasslands and deserts. The goats adapted to this ecological environment are not only large in numbers, 1,228,000 by the end of 1999, but also of fine breeds. The goats of Rutog County, in particular, are among the finest species of Tibetan goat. They are small and sturdy in build, compact and well-proportioned in the trunk, broad in the forehead and straight in the nose-bridge. Both the males and the females have horns and broad chests. An adult goat usually stands about 50 cm in height and weighs over 20 kg. The goats of Rutog are also highly valued for the high quality and workability of their cashmere wool.

China is the largest producer and exporter of cashmere wool in the world, with the annual output ranging between 8,000 and 10,000 tons and accounting for 70 percent of world total. China also tops the world in the quality of cashmere wool. However, the quality in China varies greatly from place to place because of different geographical locations and eco-climatic conditions. The cashmere wool produced in the Ngari area tops the world in the purity of strain, luster and fineness of its fibers, and is in great demand on the international market.

Since the early 1980s, the output of cashmere wool in the Ngari area has kept rising year by year, and reached 216.6 tons in 1999, accounting for one third of Tibet's total.

Cashmere products are expensive textiles, popularly known as "soft gold" and in great demand. Now China has shifted from being a mere raw material supplier to being a producer of finished goods, along with the import of foreign processing technologies and advanced equipment. As a result, the varieties, patterns and specifications of Chinese cashmere products have kept expanding, while their quality has kept improving.

The output of cashmere wool in the world is not expected to grow significantly due to the special nature of its production, and it will probably continue to stay at the level of 14,000 tons a year. Chinese cashmere products promise broad prospects on the international market. Meanwhile, domestic demand is rising along with the country's swift economic development and rising living standards. Sales of cashmere products have been increasing at a rate of 20-25 percent a year. Besides Ngari Prefecture, cashmere wool production bases have been set up in Rutog, Ge'gyai and Gerze counties.

In addition, the work to improve the breeds of goats in other parts of Tibet by crossbreeding them with Rutog goats has a bright future. In the inaccessible outlying areas, castrated male goats are used as means of conveyance in the "salt for grain" trade with other areas. Generally, a goat can carry a load of 7-10 kg and travel for months on a long-distance round trip, at a daily rate of 15-16 km. Goats also provide the local people with meat, milk and skins.

Four

THE HIMALAYAS

I. Mighty Mountain Range

Standing on the southern edge of the Qinghai-Tibet Plateau, the Himalaya Mountain range is the highest mountain system in the world. It starts from the Pamir range in the west and ends at the Bend of the Great Canyon on the lower reaches of the Yarlung Zangbo, extending more than 2,400 km in total length between the Tibet Autonomous Region of China on the one hand and India, Nepal, Sikkim and Bhutan on the other. It forms a curve protruding to the south, with its main part lying in China. In the Tibetan language, "Himalaya" means "land of ice and snow."

This mountain range has an average altitude of 6,000 m, and a continuous array of high peaks exceeding 8,000 m west of Yadong (Chomo), among which Mount Qomolangma, lying 8,848.13 m above sea level between China and Nepal is the highest peak in the world. At the northern foot of the Himalayas, the Yarlung Zangbo flows from west to east, and, as it turns south at a point near 95° E, cuts off the Himalayas to form deep gorges.

The Himalayas are the youngest as well as the highest mountain range in the world. "Himalaya" in Sanskrit means "residence of snow" while Tibetans

Springtime in the Himalayas.

call the range the "snowy mountains." This mountain system is made up of several roughly parallel mountain ranges, with its main range, the Greater Himalayas, starting from Mount Nanga Parbat (8,125 m.) in Kashmir outside China in the west, and extending along the southern edge of the Tibetan plateau in an eastward direction to Mount Namjagbarwa (7,782 m) near the Great Bend of the Yarlung Zangbo. Some geologists have likened the peaks at the two ends to two "ground nodes," which, like nails, peg the Himalayas on the southern edge of the Qinghai-Tibet Plateau, and fix the Eurasian Plate firmly on the Indian Plate. The Himalayas are 200-300 km in width, roughly with a west-east orientation. More than 50 peaks each exceeding 7,000 m above sea level stand along the curve of the mountain body that protrudes to the south. Ten of the world's 14 peaks with an altitude of 8,000 m and more are located there. Among them is the pyramid-shaped Mount Qomolangma, which is the highest point on the Earth. This cluster of towering peaks is a natural wonder that cannot be seen elsewhere in the world. The Himalayas are extensively covered with glaciers, which moisten vast expanses of land on the northern and southern flanks. The trees and waterfalls of the southern slopes add to the diversity of the scenery. The northern slopes feature snowy highlands and green grasslands dotted with lakes.

The continuous array of high peaks in the Himalayas is a barrier to the wet air currents from the Indian Ocean. As a result, the southern slopes are lush green because of ample precipitation, in sharp contrast to the northern slopes, which are under thin and sparse vegetation because of aridity. Moreover, as the altitude rises, the natural mountain scenery changes continually, so as to show a clear differentiation of natural altitudinal belts. For example, a rise in elevation from a river valley at 2,000 m to the summit of a peak exceeding 8,000 m, although the two points may be only several dozen km apart as the crow flies, can result in a quick succession of natural scenes: lush evergreen broadleaf trees in the warm and humid area at the foot of the mountains;

conifers taking the place of broadleaf trees as the altitude rises and the climate turns colder; trees giving way to shrubs as the climate gets too cold for trees to grow; meadows and then lichen taking over; and at the top, permanent ice- and snow-cover. That is to say, if one travels from the foot of a mountain to its top, one will see, on the way, a whole range of natural scenes as if journeying from the subtropical zone to the frigid North Pole.

On May 25, 1960, Chinese mountaineers scaled Mount Qomolangma from the northern slope. They surveyed the geological and physical features of the highest point on the earth.

II. Mount Qomolangma—the "Third Goddess"

Mount Qomolangma is located on the border between the Tibet Autonomous Region and the Kingdom of Nepal, covering an area of 33,819 sq km between 27°48'-29°19' N and 84°27'-88° E. The Chinese portion of Mount Qomolangma is located in Tingri, Gyirong, Nyalam and Dinggye counties under the jurisdiction of the Xigaze Prefecture.

Mount Qomolangma, the main peak of the Himalayas, is the world's highest peak, and stands 8,848.13 m above sea level. It commands the earth's highest point, towering majestically above all other mountains.

There are 548 glaciers of all sizes in a 5,000-sq-km area around Mount Qomolangma. The glaciers total 1,600 sq km. There are 217 glaciers on the northern slopes, the better-known ones being Rongpu, Gechongba, Gyabulha and Lanpa. These glaciers mostly have ice pinnacles.

Since ancient times the Tibetan people have regarded Mount Qomolangma

Mount Qomolangma.

as a holy mountain. The venerable monk Milaraspa, a solitary hermit who dwelt for nine years in a cave on Mount Qomolangma, wrote many poems in praise of the peak. One of them reads, in part: "The triangular majestic snow-covered mountain soars into the sky / Her roc-like head sporting crystal ornaments / Which shine with brilliance; / Above her float white clouds / Her head fluttering gently in their midst / Below her are multi-colored rainbows / While the cliffs at the waist of the mountain sway their sapphire-like eyebrows...." In Tibetan legends, Mount Qomolangma and the four other high peaks on its flanks are regarded as the "five sisters of longevity," with Mount Qomolangma being the "Third Goddess," "Goddess Queen" and "Goddess of Auspiciousness and Longevity" (Jomu Cering Mar). In Tibetan Buddhist paintings, the goddess is represented as a figure in white, riding a white lion and holding a golden, nine-tipped pestle in her right hand and a long

Buddhist vase in her left hand, graceful, wise and courageous.

The Rongpu Monastery on the northern slope of Mount Qomolangma, at an altitude of 5,000 m, is the highest temple in the world. It serves as the base camp for expeditions to the northern slope. On a clear day, a mass of milk-white clouds or a white band of clouds can often be seen fluttering like a flag over the mountain top, which is the "banner cloud" of meteorology. The clouds above the summit of Mount Qomolangma are the highest banner clouds in the world. Changeable and varied, they sometimes resemble a banner fluttering in strong winds, sometimes surging waves, sometimes a galloping horse and sometimes a rippling sea of clouds.

Banner clouds over Mount Qomolangma usually appear after sunrise, and are most numerous between 11 a.m. and 4 p.m. After that, because of the development of tropospheric clouds, the peak is shrouded in cloud, and becomes visible one moment and invisible the next.

Most parts of the Rongpu Glacier above 7,000 m are naked deep-brown rock slopes and gravel, which receive a large amount of solar radiation heat during the day, and the remarkable updraft thus formed sends the water vapor from the ice and snow cover at 7,000 m in altitude up to the sky to provide the necessary water for cloud formation. The height of the peak is precisely the height at which the water vapor condenses into feathery clouds hanging over the peak.

Based on the changes of the banner clouds over Mount Qomolangma, quite accurate local weather forecasts can be made. Banner clouds in an east-by-north wind will indicate that there will be two to three fine days with light winds, which is suitable for climbing; developed banner clouds over the peak indicate that the upper wind is not strong, and rain will fall within the coming two or three days; when the wind wafts the banner clouds gently in a south-

A typical Himalayan glacier.

east-northwest direction, the weather is generally not suitable for climbing; when clouds keep moving from the southwest flank of the peak to merge with the banner clouds, it indicates that generally there will be at least three days of fine weather with weak winds; and when westerly banner clouds move very swiftly, any attempt to reach the peak should be cancelled.

Mount Qomolangma and other nearby high peaks, such as Mount Qowowuyag and Mount Xixabangma, have an ice-and-snow cover of 2,712.52 sq km. Mount Qomolangma alone has 271 glaciers on its northern slope and 331 on its southern slope. The biggest one on the northern slope, the Rongpu Glacier, is a compound valley glacier as a result of the merging of several glaciers. It is 22.2 km long and covers 88.89 sq km. Its snowline is at 5,800 m, and the end of its tongue is at 5,154 m. On it, between 5,360 and 5,800 m in altitude, lie "forests" of ice pinnacles, which constitute one of the geographical wonders of Tibet and are rarely seen elsewhere in the world. Among them the "forest" of ice pinnacles of the East Rongpu Glacier is the most beautiful and most special natural scene among the medium-low-latitude mountain glacier areas in the world. Ranging between 40 and 50 m, these pinnacles are shaped like sharp swords thrust into the sky, or assume the shapes of camels, stalagmites, walls or curtains.

Moreover, this is also an area with the richest varieties of glacial and periglacial features in the world, such as glaciated landforms (cirque, cuchilla, horn, U-shaped gully, embossed rock, etc.,) ice drifts and aqueoglacial accumulation landforms (hillock moraine, lateral ridge dyke, end moraine dyke, drum, aqueoglacial fan and lake, back furrow, etc.,) and periglacial features as a result of ablation from freezing and gravitation (stone pillar, earth pillar, lithic apron, stone sea, stone river, landslide, stone dyke, stone belt and multilateral stone ring). Indeed, this area can be called a "glacier museum."

The section of the Himalayas in the Mount Qomolangma area is subject not only to control by the east-west strike of the main structure, but also to control by the north-north-east strike and south-south-west strike of a number of structures, so that the main mountain range is cut from east to west into the Zenagangri, Yangrangangri-Tapulegangri and Gudanggangri-Bailigangri mountain ranges. Among them lie the Pum Qu, Rongxar Qu, Boqu, Gyirong Zangbo and Dougar rivers, which flow in a north—south direction along deep gorges formed as a result of structural rift and erosion. These rivers feature swift, torrential currents, steep drop and numerous waterfalls. Since these valleys are passages for moist air currents moving from south to north, the valleys along the lower reaches have a well-developed forest ecological system on the southern Himalayan slope and boast rich hydropower potential.

The northern Himalayan slope features gently rising broad mountain valleys and lake-basins, with the plateau surface at an average altitude of approximately 4,300 m. The Tingri and Xixabangma grasslands are good grazing grounds. There are quite a few inland lakes and marshlands here, with the main lakes being Paiku Co, Langqiang Co, Helin Co and Chuocolung Co. During the middle and late Pleistocene period, these lakes were interlinked lakes, which gradually shrank and broke up into smaller ones because of the swift uplifting of the Himalayas and the drying of the plateau. The biggest lake here now is Paiku Co, covering about 300 sq km and located 4,595 m above sea level.

III. Rich Altitudinal Eco-System

Thanks to its unique favorable geographical location and natural conditions, the Mount Qomolangma area has a complex and diverse eco-system and rich biological resources. Preliminary surveys show that there are 2,348 species of higher plants and 278 species of animals here, a dozen of which are listed as rare wild animals under state protection. Meanwhile, Mount Qomolangma's great

Altitudinal belts of the Himalayas.

height difference (the highest point being 8,848.13 m and the lowest, 1,440 m) and the climatic difference between the southern and northern slopes have resulted in special altitudinal ecological combinations of the southern and northern slopes, with many different natural landscapes. Within the few km from Zham to Mount Qomolangma, one is able to sample a complete spectrum of natural belts from the subtropical to the Arctic, and a variety of diverse ecological scenes.

The southern part of the Mount Qomolangma area, including that lying beyond Chinese territory, belongs to the humid mountain forest eco-system of the Himalayan southern slope, which is a complex eco-system with a low mountain rain forest eco-system as its basis and formed of eight altitudinal ecological combinations. There are six main altitudinal belts within the Chinese section of the Mount Qomolangma area, with their landscape features being an eco-system of mountain evergreen and semi-evergreen broadleaf forests and evergreen conifers, distributed between 900 and 2,600 m above sea level. The slopes of the valleys in this area are steep, forming unfathomable gorges and large numbers of waterfalls. The climate is warm and humid, and the annual average temperature ranges between 10 and 20 degrees centigrade, with the average being 16-20 degrees centigrade in the warmest month and 15-1 degrees centigrade in the coldest. The frost-free period lasts for 250 days, the annual precipitation is 1,000-2,000 mm, and there is much mist and cloud. The vegetation consists of subtropical evergreen, semi-evergreen broadleaf forests and evergreen conifers. There is a rich variety of wildlife, mostly oriental-realm subtropical forest animals. The soil is mainly of mountain yellow-brown soil, and its layer is 50 to 60 cm thick. Two crops are reaped a year, and paddy rice can be grown in the lowest places.

The eco-system of mountain warm temperate zone evergreen conifers and hard-leaf evergreen broadleaf forests lies between 2,400 and 3,300 m above sea level. The climate in this area is warm-cool and humid, with an average annual temperature of 7-10 degrees centigrade, a frost-free period of 150-250 days and a wide difference in precipitation between the eastern and western parts. The valleys along the lower reaches of the Pum Qu River, the Rongxar Valley and the Boqu Valley in the east receive 2,000-2,500 mm of rain a year, while the Gyirong Zangbo-Dougar area in the west has an annual rainfall of 1,000-1,500 mm. The vegetation is Chinese hemlock, pine and hard-leaf evergreen oak forests. The soil is mainly mountain acid brown soil, fertile and

The river valley farming region in Gyirong County of the southern Himalayas.

thick. The main crops are qingke (barley), wheat, potatoes and rape. Two crops of qingke are harvested a year. The area is also suitable for cultivating apple, pear, peach and apricot trees.

The eco-system of sub-highland cold temperate dark conifers and deciduous broadleaf trees located at 3,100-3,900 m above sea level. The climate is cool, pleasant and humid, and the average annual temperature is 2.5-7 degrees centigrade, with the average in the warmest month being 10-14 degrees centigrade and that of the coldest month being 5 degrees below zero centigrade. The frost-free period is 90-150 days, and the annual rainfall is 1,000-2,000 mm. Snow falls between October and May next year, with the average snow cover being 60-180 cm. The main vegetation is fir and birch. The dominant animals are Palaearctic. The soil is mainly dark-brown and grey. Farmland is scanty, and villages are few.

The eco-system of mountain sub-frigid shrubs and meadows is distributed between 3,700 m and 4,700 m above sea level. The climate is cold and humid, and the average annual temperature is only 2.5-2 degrees centigrade below zero, with the temperature in the warmest month being 6-10 degrees centigrade and that in the coldest month being 5-10 degrees centigrade below zero. The annual precipitation is 500-1,000 mm, and snow falls between September and June next year, with a snow cover of 20 cm to 50 cm. The soil is sub-alpine shrub-meadow soil and alpine meadow soil. The eco-system consists of two subsystems, that is, highland sub-frigid shrubs and alpine frigid meadows. The former has a variety of azaleas as its dominant groups, mainly Wight azalea, snow-layer azalea, setose azalea and seven other varieties of azalea. During May and June every year, the area is a riot of azalea blooms. The frigid alpine meadows have good vegetation, the commonly seen herbaceous plants being alpine sagebrush, knotweed, round spike knotweed, sheep fescue, Himalayan sagebrush, common green reed and a variety of winter jasmine. When summer comes, flowers dot the green grasslands. In addition, the area abounds in valuable medicinal herbs, such as Chinese caterpillar fungus, bulb of fritillary and *Figwortflower Picrorhiza*. This eco-system features local summer grazing grounds suitable for seasonal grazing.

The frigid alpine ice margin eco-system lies between 4,700 m and 5,900 m above sea level. There, the climate is extremely harsh, and the average annual temperature is 2-6 degrees centigrade below zero, with the temperature in the coldest month being 5-16 degrees centigrade below zero. The frost-free period is 0-90 days and the main form of precipitation is solid. The bottom of the soil is a permanent frozen layer while the top layer is primitive soil frequently alternating between melting during the day and freezing at night. It is coarse and full of gravel, with an extremely low content of clay fraction. The vegetation consists of short and sparse cushion-shaped plants. The most common animals are mountain goats, grey-necked rat-rabbits, Himalayan rat-rabbits and snow leopards. This belt sees little human presence and remains basically primitive.

The alpine frigid ice-and-snow eco-system lies between 5,500 m and 8,848.13 m above sea level, and is the world's highest, and the harshest in terms of ecological environment. This zone is even less known than the North and South Poles. It is estimated that the average annual temperature is 6 degrees centigrade below zero. A Chinese mountaineering expedition recorded a temperature of 30 degrees centigrade below zero on the summit of Mount Qomolangma at 4:20 on May 25, 1960, and it is estimated that the absolute temperature could drop to 60 degrees centigrade below zero. The annual precipitation is probably below 500 mm, all in solid state. Except for the steep cliffs and the wind-swept mountaintops, most parts of the area are covered with perpetual ice and snow. In spite of this, life exists there. The Chinese expedition spotted a kind of gentian at 6,100 m above sea level and germs were collected from among pebbles at 8,306 m above sea level. This eco-system is one least affected by human activity in the world. With the exception of a small number of peaks that have been visited by climbers, most areas have preserved their primitive natural features well and are ideal places for the study of the origin of life and the adaptability of life to an extreme environment.

In order to protect the unique eco-systems of the Mount Qomolangma area and its resources of rare wild animals and plants, the Qomolangma National Nature Reserve was set up in 1988. Covering 38,000 sq km, it is the third-largest nature reserve in Tibet, after Changtang and Xainza, and one of the nature reserves with the highest altitude in the world.

IV. Enthusiasm for Mountain Climbing

As early as in 1717 (the 56th year of the reign of Qing Emperor Kangxi), Mount Qomolangma's name was already marked on Chinese maps. The Chinese transliteration used at that time was "Zhumu Langma Alin," "Zhumu" being the name of a Tibetan goddess, "langma" meaning third among brothers or sisters, and "alin" meaning a peak in the Manchu language. The standardised name "Qomolangma" did not emerge until the founding of the People's Republic of China in 1949.

Starting in the early 19th century, Mount Qomolangma has attracted climbers and scientists from all over the world. At 11:30 a.m. on May 29, 1953, Edmund Hillary, a member of a British mountaineering expedition, and his Sherpa guide Tensing became the first humans to reach the peak, the highest point on the earth. On May 25, 1960, Wang Fuzhou, Goinbo and Qu Yinhua, members of a Chinese mountaineering team, became the first climbers to success-

On the way to an ice-pinnacle area.

Mountaineers' campsite at the foot of Mount Qomolangma.

fully scale the peak from the northeast ridge.

In 1964, ten members of a Chinese mountaineering team surmounted the 8,012-meter-high Mount Xixabangma, the hitherto only unconquered peak among all the 14 peaks in the world that exceed 8,000 m in altitude.

In 1988, a three-nation (China, Japan and Nepal) expedition climbed Mount Qomolangma, conducting for the first time a two-way (north-south and south-north simultaneously) crossing of the peak. A total of close to 300 people were involved in the support work on both flanks of the mountain. Japan's NHK set up a satellite ground station at the base camp on the northern slope, to provide live coverage of the climb, also a first. On May 5, 12 climbers from the three countries reached the summit. Four of them were Chinese: Tsering Doje, Li Zhixin, Rinchen Puncog and Tsering Doje Senior.

By the end of 1990, a total of 267 climbers in 53 expeditions from 26 countries had reached this highest peak in the world; and in the five decades by the end of November 2002, the number of such climbers had totalled to 1,200. They had discovered and opened 42 routes leading to the summit.

Every year, expeditions from different parts of the world assemble at the Rongpu Monastery at the foot of Mount Qomolangma, and set up their camps for assaults on the summit, the "third pole" of the Earth. In 2003, the 50th anniversary of the first successful ascent of Mount Qomolangma, scores of expeditions from all over the world gathered on its south and north slopes to mark the event. Fourteen Chinese climbers, either as members of the Sino-Korean Joint Expedition or the Chinese Expedition, reached the top on May 21 and 22, respectively. By then, a total of 61 Chinese climbers had reached the summit on a total of 14 occasions over 43 years.

Five

THE BEAUTIFUL AND RICHLY ENDOWED YARLUNG ZANGBO

The Yarlung Zangbo-Brahmaputra River flows through China, India and Bangladesh, with some of its tributaries originating in and flowing through Sikkim and Bhutan. It is a large Asian river as well as a well-known international river. Flowing for 3,350 km, it has a drainage area of about 666,000 sq km. The section of the river within China, 2,057 km long and 240,000 sq km in drainage area, is called the Yarlung Zangbo. The average altitude of the Yarlung Zangbo valley is 4,500 m. The trunk river of the Yarlung Zangbo can be divided into the upper, middle and lower reaches in terms of topographical features and volume of water.

—The Upper Reaches The portion of the river from its source to Legze at Saga constitutes the upper reaches. This portion, including the source section, is 268 km long, with a fall of 1,190 m, or an average gradient of 4.45 per thousand. The source section is called the Maquan River (Damqog Zangbo), which rises in the Gyimayangzong Glacier on the northern slope of the middle section of the Himalayas, at an altitude of 5,590 m. In the area of the source

The Yarlung Zangbo River.

section, there are many drift lakes, which are mostly linked by rivers. The valley from the source to Legze, at an altitude of 4,800-4,500 m, is flat and broad, with a well-developed meander, an unruly river course and an extensive distribution of marshes and wetlands. Because of aridity, the area, expansive alpine pastures, is sparsely populated

—The Middle Reaches The middle reaches are from Legze at Saga, at an altitude of 4,500 m, to Paiqu, at an altitude of 2,800 m. This portion is 1,293 km long, with a fall of 1,520 m, or an average gradient of 1.18 per thousand. The valley is now broad and now narrow, so that broad valleys alternate with basins and gorges, the major ones of the latter being the Dazhuka, Zetang and Gyaca gorges. The gorges are on average 100 m wide at the floor and 40 to 300 km long, with the width of the water surface being 50 m. The water is torrential, with a big fall, so there is great potential for hydropower. The

Gyaca Gorge is the most famous of the gorges. It is 37.2 km. long, but the water surface is only 30 to 40 m wide. The steep mountains on both banks tower over 500 m above the river. It has a fall of approximately 270 m, with an average gradient of 7.26 per thousand. Larger valleys consist of terraces and valley flats, such as the Xigaze Strath, the Quxu Strath and Nyingchi Strath, which are from two to seven km wide. The water table gradient is generally below 1.0 per thousand, so that the water flows slowly, and there are many shoals, sandbanks and prongs. These wide valleys are the main farming areas in Tibet. The silt and other sediment carried by the main stream of the river, under the conditions of the strong westerlies during the winter half of the year and the superposition of circulating currents in the mountain valleys, have turned into developed valley deserts, which are distributed like an intermittent belt along the valley. The main tributaries along this section are the Nyangqu, Lhasa (Gyi Qu) and Nyang rivers.

Namjagbarwa Peak.

—The Lower Reaches, the Canyon of the Great Bend The river course below Paiqu forms a great bend as it flows in a north-easterly direction around the 7,782-m-high Mount Namjagbarwa. It continues on in a south-westerly and then south-easterly direction. This canyon extends 496.3 km in length, with an average depth of 2,268 m, making it the longest and deepest gorge in the world. The mountains on both sides are dangerously steep and covered with thick forests, while the river below roars on torrentially, with tremendous hydropower potential. Field surveys have established the location of the narrowest point of the Great Canyon somewhere between Ganglang and Dabo, near the start of the Great Canyon. It is 75 m wide and the speed of the river's current is 10 m per second. The most dangerously steep section is from Daduka to Bangbo at Medog, a distance of 240 km. The river course is 80-200 m wide here, with a fall of 2,600 m. The main tributary along the lower reaches is Parlung Zangbo.

The Yarlung Zangbo valley is a very unique geographical region, and has a very diverse eco-system. Its level of diversification of species, in particular, has an important place in China. These species include mosses, terrestrial vertebrate animals, fish, fungus and insects. The Mount Qomolangma, Medog and Yarlung Zangbo Great Canyon nature reserves are among the largest of their kind in China. The valley is immensely rich in sunshine and water resources, and hydropower. The rich forest resources along the valley are mainly distributed on the middle and lower reaches of the main river, and they play a very important role in regulating the water source.

This area is the cradle of the brilliant Tibetan culture, and a holy place of Tibetan Buddhism. It embraces the Potala Palace, Tashilunpo Monastery and many other famous sites of historical interest. The world's highest peak, Mount Qomolangma, and the world's biggest gorge, the Yarlung Zangbo Great Canyon, are places of great appeal to explorers the world over.

The valley is a multi-ethnic area with Tibetans as the dominant ethnic group. There are also people of the Han, Hui, Moinba and other ethnic groups. It is among the most sparsely populated areas in China, averaging four persons per sq km.

The area formed by the Yarlung Zangbo and its two major tributaries, the Lhasa and Nyangqu rivers, on the middle reaches, is popularly known as the "Area of One River Plus Two Tributaries." It is endowed with very favorable natural conditions. The straths of the mainstream and tributaries are 5-10 km. wide, and the land is flat and well irrigated. The solar radiation is strong, and there are many hours of sunshine, a wide range of temperature in a 24-hour-period and a long growing period for crops. There is an abundance of water resources, and the total annual runoff of the rivers amounts to 23.4 billion cu m, averaging approximately 30,776 cu m per person, far higher than the national average. Moreover, the quality of the water is superb. The farmland

Explorers crossing the Yarlung Zangbo River.

totals 176,000 ha, which accounts for more than half of the total of the Tibet Autonomous Region, and averages 0.132 ha per person. Hydro, geothermal, solar and wind energy sources are abundant, and the conditions for development are favorable. The reserve of hydropower is 5,941 megawatts. The area is the most densely populated in Tibet due to higher urbanisation, with its population making up 36 percent of the Autonomous Region's total and averaging 12 persons per sq km. It has fairly convenient communication and transportation facilities and, by and large, enjoys a good investment environment.

Yet, the ecological environment of the Yarlung Zangbo Valley is fragile, and the area is prone to natural calamities such as desertification, earthquakes and landslides. This factor has restricted the development of the area to a great extent.

Fishing in a raft made of yak hide in the middle reaches of the Yarlung Zangbo River.

I. The Hanging River—the Mother River of Tibetans

The Yarlung Zangbo originates from the Gyimayangzong Glacier on the northern slope of the middle section of the Himalayas in the southwestern part of the Tibet Autonomous Region. It flows from west to east between the Himalayas and the Gangdise-Nyainqentanglha Range, and makes a southward turn at a point east of Paiqu in Mainling County. It ranks fifth among China's major rivers in terms of length and drainage area, third after the Yangtze and Pearl rivers in terms of average annual flow, which amounts to 4,425 cu m per second, and second after the Yangtze in terms of natural hydropower reserves, which exceed 100,000 megawatts.

Approximately three-fourths of the entire Yarlung Zangbo is located over 3,000 m above sea level, and one-third at an altitude exceeding 4,000 m. This fact is unique among the world's larger rivers and has rightly earned it the nickname of " hanging river".

As it flows from west to east, the Yarlung Zangbo receives five major tributaries — the Dogxung Zangbo, Nyangqu River, Lhasa River, Nyang River and Parlung Zangbo — and numerous smaller ones. Its expansive drainage area boasts alpine tundra covered by perpetual snow; alpine cold strath grasslands dotted with lakes and swamps; warm, semi-arid valley bushvelds with abundant fertile farmland; and evergreen subtropical and tropical mountain forests (dark conifers, evergreen broadleaf trees and monsoon forests). Its varied landscapes combine the charms of the various types of scenery to be found south of the Yangtze River in East China and, more importantly, the primitive and wild touches of the highlands. The Yarlung Zangbo valley abounds in natural resources. Apart from various animals and plants, and stretches of forests and grasslands, its inexhaustible solar energy, hydropower and reserves of chromite are all bounties bestowed by Nature on the valley, and constitute an important material foundation for the sustainable economic development of the Tibetan highlands.

The Yarlung Zangbo, from its riverhead to its end, growing from drops of melted snow and ice into tiny streams and then into a mighty, torrential river, nurtures the grasslands along the Maquan River, irrigates large tracts of fertile farmland in the area of "one river plus two tributaries," and moistens the thick forests in the Nyang River-Parlung Zangbo Valley. Thanks to the favorable natural ecological environment and rich and varied natural resources for agriculture, and on top of that, the hard-working Tibetan people, the valley has been turned into the "granary of Tibet," with developed agriculture and

A river valley in southern Tibet.

animal husbandry and an abundance of products. It is also where the major towns of the Autonomous Region are located — Lhasa, Xigaze, Gyangze, Zetang, Nyingchi and Bayi. It has a population of nearly one million, and large tracts of farmland, accounting for about half of the total population and farmland of Tibet. In other words, the valley, accounting for less than one fifth of the total area of Tibet, supports more than half of its population. Therefore, the valley of the Yarlung Zangbo is an ideal place for the Tibetan people to proliferate and prosper, and the river is the "mother river" that has nurtured them. In addition, as the political, economic and cultural center of the Tibetan plateau, and the birthplace of the Tibetan ethnic group, it has a brilliant culture and history of civilisation dating back several thousand years.

II. The Spectacular "Braided Water Systems" and Deserts in the "Land of Snow"

One leaves the source of the Yarlung Zangbo River, goes through the high, expansive and wide straths of the Maquan River, then turns east along the river, and soon reaches the seat of Zhongba County, a small inconspicuous border town. "Zhongba" in Tibetan means the "land of oxen," as if to remind people that the area used to be the country where wild yaks roamed. Nowadays, they can hardly be spotted around the county seat, because of traffic and human movement.

The county seat of Zhongba was moved to the present site in recent years, because the original one had to be deserted as many of the dwellings and roads there had been buried by advancing sand dunes. This picture of human beings retreating before advancing sand on the roof of the world provides much food for thought, and deserves serious study. On the one hand, it reflects the process of changes in the natural environment characterized by the drying of the climate on the plateau in recent years and the continuously expanding desertification; on the other, isn't the human factor also behind the worsening of the environment? Studies show that the human factor, in such activities as overgrazing, that has led to the degeneration of the natural grasslands cannot be ruled out, although it is a local and not the leading cause.

One leaves the county seat, goes south, and soon gets to the confluence of the Maquan River and its tributary on its northern side, the Ca Qu. One goes east from there, and gets to the middle reaches of the Yarlung Zangbo. Under the influence of the geological structures and because of the differing hardness and resistance of the rocks on the banks against erosion, the valley below Legze is now broad and now narrow. Even the straths there, with fewer prongs and swamps, are not as wide and flat as those on the upper reaches.

The valley flats along Yarlung Zangbo east of Legze, although somewhat narrower, are still natural pastures formed by broad shoal land and torrential accumulation platforms on both sides of the valley bottom. Black felt tents of Tibetan herdsmen are scattered here and there. Herds of cattle and flocks of sheep graze leisurely on luxuriant grass. It is still a scene typical of the alpine pastures, only that there are more herdsmen as a result of a more developed animal husbandry than on the upper reaches. This part of the autonomous region lies close to the national boundary, and nationals of China's friendly neighbor, Nepal, often come through some passes in the Himalayas to the south of the Yarlung Zangbo and camp there to engage in barter trade in grain, tea, meat, butter, wool and salt with local Tibetans.

The seat of Saga County, on the northern bank of the Yarlung Zangbo, is at an altitude of approximately 4,400 m. But the area is warmer than Zhongba and Legze on the upper stream. Saga has pockets of farming, allowed by local climate, although animal husbandry is still the dominant economic sector there. In Tibet, because of the special ground thermal effects of the plateau and the strong solar radiation through the dry and clean air, crops can grow at a very high altitude, often showing an astonishingly good performance in such a micro-climatic environments as valleys and basins. For example, the upper limit for spring *qingke* is 4,750 m, and for cold-resistant, coolness-loving crops like winter wheat, potato, rape and peas, it is 4,300 m, 4,650 m and 4,450 m, respectively, far higher than the upper limits for growing such crops in other parts of China or the rest of the world. For example, the upper limit for growing wheat in eastern Mexico is only 3,050 m above sea level. Even in Xainza, Gerze and other places on the northern Tibet plateau, where it is even colder and harsher, *qingke* can be grown on a small scale in valleys or basins at an altitude of about 4,600 m. Of course, owing to insufficient ground warmth and frequent frost spells, harvests in some high-altitude areas, including Saga, are not stable, as they are highly dependent on the weather. Good harvests are possible only in a year of favorable weather. Therefore, such high-altitude farming is limited mainly to valleys below 4,100 m above sea level. For example, only the areas around Xigaze and Lhasa can be sure of stable harvests, and, with better field management, can reap bumper harvests. In short, Saga County can be said to be the westernmost limit of the farming area throughout the Yarlung Zangbo valley. The areas west of Saga are exclusively pastoral.

An interesting picture to be seen in the farmland near Saga is the way local farmers plow the land. Two strong, black yaks pull a plow shoulder to shoulder, with the yoke, a thick round wooden pole linked to the long shaft of the plow, tied with ropes to the yaks' horns instead of mounted on their shoulders in the normal way. Local people explain that the horns of a yak are where its strength is concentrated, and are therefore used to pull a plow, the same way as a bull uses its horns in a bullfight. Such an explanation sounds plausible, and reflects the admiration of the Tibetan people for the awesome prowess associated with the horns of the yak, and their preference for the traditional way of using the yaks as draught animals.

At a point several km east of Saga, the already broad strath becomes even wider, as the tributaries join the mainstream, and the triangular valley basin is 7-8 km wide. The riverbed is flat, and the river course branches off into many prongs, which now join and now separate. The sandbanks lying between them are also joined and broken on and off, so that they are braided together into an irregular shape like a girl's braided hair. This is one of the special features of the river course on the middle reaches of the Yarlung Zangbo, so-called "anastomosed drainage." Although such a phenomenon can also be seen on the upstream, the braided water system is even more typical and grander in scale after the river flows in an easterly direction through

An aerial view of a braided water system in a wide valley floor at the central section of the Yarlung Zangbo.

A wide valley floor of the Lhasa River.

more than 200 km of narrow valleys and gorges that are almost linked to one another, and reaches the wide valley of the mainstream of the Yarlung Zangbo north of Xigaze and the Quxu-Zetang area. Because the slopes on both sides of the mainstream and its tributaries in this area have scanty vegetation and are seriously eroded, the great amount of soil the river carries is mostly deposited in the river when the riverbed turns wider and the flow of the water slows down. For example, more than 780,000 tons of silt is deposited annually in the Quxu-Zetang section. This is most serious in the delta where the two major tributaries, the Nyangqu and Lhasa rivers, meet the Yarlung Zangbo. The silt has raised the riverbed, which hampers the flow of the water. Therefore, in the low-water season during the winter half of the year, as the water level drops, a large number of sandbanks emerge above the water surface, and the entire river floor is all but covered by a braided riverbed. The giant braided water system thus formed, 3-5 km wide, 8-10 km long, is a spectacular sight. But when the rainy season comes in summer, the river is in spate, and the valley floor turns into a vast expanse of water, submerging most of the sandbanks. Travelers on the Sino-Nepalese International Highway leading to Lhasa, Xigaze and Kathmandu will invariably pass over the Quxu Bridge, which straddles the Yarlung Zangbo at this point. Whenever they cross the bridge, they cannot help but marvel at the sight of the braided waterway.

The wide, gently descending riverbed of the Yarlung Zangbo, with multiple bends, is a favorable breeding ground for fish. The river has a greater number of fish and more varieties than any other river on the plateau. Common varieties of fish to be found along its middle reaches are some endemic species of Schizothorocic carp and double lip carp, while Medog loaches are only to be found in the Great Canyon on the lower reaches of the river. In addition to their anal scales, these varieties also have fine scales on their bodies, hence the name "fine-scale fish."

As the middle section of the Yarlung Zangbo passes eastward through the Daju Gorge, east of Saga, the valley continues to maintain its widening tendency until it reaches the Zetang area of Shannan Prefecture. In a striking contrast to the spectacular braided water system of the river are undulating chains of crescent-shaped sand dunes lining the banks. These chains stretch on and off for several hundred km, and are sometimes broken by lower sand ridges, grid-shaped sand dunes and sand mounds that stand only 1-2 m high.

But how can such a desert scene appear on the "roof of the world," known for its subnival climate?This has much to do with the special natural conditions prevalent along the middle reaches of the Yarlung Zangbo in terms of climate, topography and hydrology. First, precipitation in this area is on the low side, and is concentrated in summer, while the winter half of the year is dominated by strong winds. Second, the flow is big, but varies greatly in the high- and low-water seasons. And third, the riverbed is seriously silted up. As a result of the joint workings of these factors, a large amount of silt has been deposited in the broad valleys on the middle reaches. The deposited silt emerges from the water as the water surface drops in the dry season and, whipped up by strong winds under the influence of the westerlies, it is swept to the banks and the slopes, where its accumulation over a long period of time has led to the desert landform as we know it today. Of course, human activity in recent years is partly responsible for damaging the original natural vegetation on the banks and slopes. For example, over-cutting of shrubs and grass for firewood, unwise reclamation of wasteland and overgrazing have reduced the ground vegetation, exposing the ground to wind and water erosion. Thus, sand is swept up at the source or is carried down the river and leads to silting in the riverbed, resulting in the above-described natural scene of the braided water system accompanied by chains of sand dunes.

Surveys by some experts show that in the valley on the middle reaches of the Yarlung Zangbo, especially within the area of "one river plus two tributaries," the total area of exposed sandy land, including shifting sand dunes, amounts to more than 112,000 ha, or the equivalent of two-thirds of the existing farmland in this area. Meanwhile, some specialists hold that the entire Qinghai-Tibet Plateau has been turning drier and warmer in recent decades as a result of global climatic changes. Against this background, the climate in the valley on the middle reaches is showing a tendency of warming up and decreasing humidity. This will aggravate desertification in this area, to the great detriment of the ecological environment and the production and livelihood of the inhabitants there. However, what is gratifying is that the local government has fully recognised the seriousness of the desertification threat, and is taking active step to hold the deserts in check. Since the project to improve the environment of the area of "one river plus two tributaries" was started in

1991, a protective forest belt, 150 km long and 700 m wide, was planted in a matter of a few years on the shoal land on the southern bank of the river from the Quxu Bridge to Zetang. Consisting mainly of Beijing poplars, Xinjiang poplars and a local poplar variety, the belt has turned about 6,700 ha of shoal land green, as the young seedlings have grown into tall trees. On the edge of the belt facing the highway, local varieties of willow have been planted. In the pilot sand-control projects carried out in some places, especially in Jangdam Township, Xigaze City, by the Yarlung Zangbo, some measures have shown certain effects with a potential for extension to other places included in the project to improve the area of "one river plus two tributaries." These measures include the use of straw grids and gravel to fix sand dunes, and afforesting sand dunes by scattering seeds and planting saplings of varieties that are suited to the sandy land, such as sagebrush, sandy knotweed, common branch sweetvetch and Korshinsk tea shrub.

III. Tibet's Granary — the "Golden Delta"

The alluvial flats on the straths along the middle reaches of the Yarlung Zangbo and the alluvial terraces on both banks provide large tracts of fertile farmland. This is even truer of the straths of its tributaries, the Nyangqu and Lhasa rivers, and of the middle section of the Yarlung Zangbo from the Quxu Bridge to Zetang. When one travels on the highway parallel to the Yarlung Zangbo, one will see what is not seen in other parts of Tibet — tract after tract of fields under *qingke* barley, winter wheat and rape. The middle and lower reaches of the Lhasa and Nyangqu rivers and their confluence with the mainstream of the Yarlung Zangbo constitute a zone with the most developed valley agriculture in Tibet, enjoying water and temperature conditions suitable for wheat crops and having a concentration of farmland. People often call this area of "one river plus two tributaries" a "golden delta" and ``Tibet's granary," as it boasts more than half of the total farmland in Tibet, and the grain it produces is enough to support four-fifths of the total population of the autonomous region.

The fact that the area of "one river plus two tributaries" is the major grain producer in this land of snows is due not only to its favorable strath terrain, ample water supply and the hard work of the local farmer, but also to its unique ecological and climatic environment. This area lies approximately between 28°-30° N, roughly on the same parallel as Chongqing, Hunan Province's capital Changsha and Dongting Lake, Jiujiang and Poyang Lake in Jiangxi Province, and Zhejiang Province's coastal cities of Hangzhou and Ningbo. At an altitude exceeding 3,400 m and lying deep in the heartland of the plateau, this area is far higher than the interior and coastal parts of China, and at a disadvantage in terms of temperature, thermal condition and precipitation when compared with the eastern areas on the same parallel. It has a highland monsoon temperate semi-arid climate, with an average annual temperature of 2.4-8.5 degrees centigrade and an annual rainfall of 270-550 mm. Under the influence of the Qinghai-Tibet westerlies in the winter half of the year, the temperature may drop to below zero centigrade, the rainfall is scanty, the wind blows hard and the air is dry. But in the other half of the year the temperature rises remarkably under the influence of the warm and humid air currents from the Indian Ocean and the Bay of Bengal, with the average temperature in July and August being 11.2-17 degrees centigrade. The amount of rainfall also increases, with the rainfall in the May-September period accounting for more than 80 percent of the annual total. The matching of rain and temperature is a climatic condition favorable for the growing of *qingke*, wheat, rape and other coolness-loving crops and provides a suitable eco-climatic environment for the agricultural production in the area of "one river plus two tributaries." The moderate summer temperature, long growing period for crops (The growth of *qingke* and wheat, from sowing, sprouting and tillering to ripening, takes almost a year) and the matching of sunshine and temperature combine to yield high outputs of *qingke* and wheat, setting a record of 900 kg per *mu* (equivalent to one-fifteenth of a ha) and making the area one of the high-yield wheat producers in the country. Agro-meteorologists have put the theoretical production potential of the farmland in the area of "one river plus two tributaries" at 700-1,400 kg per *mu*. In other words, given greater input in terms of water, soil and seed improvement, field management, and science and technology, per-unit output could rise considerably from the present level of only 200 kg per *mu* and gradually approach this theoretical production potential.

IV. Lhasa, the Holy City

The Lhasa River originates in the Nyainqentanglha Mountains, and flows for 551 km. This river, the largest tributary of the Yarlung Zangbo, drains an area of 32,500 sq km, or 13.5 percent of the total drainage area of the Yarlung Zangbo water system. From its source 5,200 m above sea level to its mouth 3,450 m above sea level, it flows through the Damxung and Painbo basins and the Lhasa Plain. With large tracts of farmland and a big population, this area is one of key centers of agricultural development in the area of "one river plus two tributaries." Located on its northern bank, Lhasa, with a history of 1,300 years, is the capital of the Tibet Autonomous Region, and the political, economic, cultural and religious center of Tibet. "Lhasa" in the Tibetan language means "holy land" or "Buddhist land." Its ancient name, "Rasa," means "goat soil." Legend has it that when Princess Wencheng of the Tang Dynasty (618-907) came to Tibet (then known as the Tubo Kingdom) to marry its king, Songtsen Gampo, in a matrimonial alliance between Tang and Tubo, what is now Lhasa was still an alluvial flat where a temple (the Jokhang Temple) was to be built beside a small lake called Ogco. The princess was not satisfied with the geomantic position of the lake and, in order to ward off supposed evil spirits, had it filled with earth carried on the backs of white goats before a new temple was built. Thus, the name of the new capital city bore the words "ra" (meaning "goat" in Tibetan) and "sa" (meaning "earth" in Tibetan). The Chinese transliteration of "Rasa" was Luosuo, which was used in history books to refer to what was later called Lhasa. Later, Princess Wencheng built the Mamoche Temple near the Jokhang Temple. The two temples were among the first large buildings in the history of Lhasa. As more and more pilgrims traveled there, quite a few inns and dwellings were built around the Jokhang Temple, and the old city area, the present-day Barkor Street, began to grow out of them. Meanwhile, Songtsen Gampo expanded the palace-castle, the Potala, on the Red Hill, so that a plateau city famous in China and the world as well began to thrive on the Lhasa Plain. At present, the city has an urban area of 523 sq km, and an urban population of approximately 130,000. Tibetans are the dominant ethnic group among the 30 represented in Lhasa, including the Han, Hui and Mongolian. Lhasa is the largest city in Tibet.

The Potala, which was first built during the seventh century, is a 13-story, castle-style structure sitting majestically on the top of the Red Hill, 115.4 m from the surrounding plain. Its structure and shape are very special and ornate. "Potala" is a transliteration of the Sanskrit word "Potalaka." The Potalaka Hill is supposed to be the residence of Avalokitesvara (gradually changed into the feminine image "Guanyin" or "Goddess of Mercy" after Buddhism was spread to China). The Potala was the official residence of the successive Dalai Lamas.

The magnificent Potala has granite outer walls, which are painted in red and white. It consists of halls and rooms of various sizes, such as prayer halls, stupa halls, shrines, a seminary and living quarters for monks. The main structures are called the White Palace and the Red Palace. The former used to be the Dalai Lama's living quarters, and his office space where he conducted his political activities. The latter is devoted to the stupas of the successive Dalai Lamas and shrines of Buddhist statues. Many cultural relics in the Potala are on show to visitors.

The Jokhang Temple is situated in the eastern part of the city. With a history of more than 1,000 years, this internationally known temple is a four-story, portico-type structure. Although not as massive or as imposing as the Potala, it is special for the introduction of architectural styles from the interior part of China as well as from such foreign countries as Nepal and India. The image of Sakyamuni in the niche of the main hall was brought by Princess Wencheng from Chang'an, present-day Xi'an. In front of the statue are incense burners and butter oil lamps, in the midst of piles of banknotes and coins tossed in by worshippers. It is said that there are some instances of pious Buddhist followers donating all their incomes from many years of hard work to temples in the hope of ascending to paradise after death or acquiring a happy next life.

In front of the Jokhang Temple can be seen pilgrims performing their rituals. They first stand upright, then prostrate themselves on the ground with both arms outstretched, repeating these movements countless times. They are mostly elderly people, and women at that. Holding a rosary (usually with 108 beads), they move one bead each time they complete one prostration, until all the beads have been moved. Some pilgrims are said to start prostrating themselves the moment they leave their homes, and continue to do so all the way to the Jokhang Temple, no matter how far away they live.

Jiefang (liberation) Park, also called Zongjiaolukang, is the second-largest park in Lhasa, after People's Park, which used to be the Dalai Lama's summer palace, the Norbulingka. Special attractions of Jiefang Park are the restful "Dragon King Pond" and the tall, bizarre-shaped willow trees, *Salix paraplesia Schneid*, that are at least 100 years old. Outside the park is a busy street market featuring stands of beef, mutton and pork, fresh vegetables and fish from the Lhasa River, as well as mountain and sea products brought from far away. Most vegetables are local produce. Greenhouses and the film-mulching cultivation technique have been used extensively in local vegetable production, taking advantage of the ample sunshine in Tibet.

Lhasa is 3,650 m above sea level, higher than Wanfoding (Thousand-Buddha Summit), the main peak of Mount Emei in Sichuan. Its average annual temperature is 7.5 degrees centigrade, with the average temperature in summer being 15 degrees centigrade and that in winter, 2.3 degrees centigrade below zero. So it is not very hot in summer and is not colder than Beijing in winter. In ordinary years, people can do without heating in winter, although it freezes at night occasionally, but by day it is pretty warm in the sun, even to the extent of feeling burnt. Sunshine hours exceed 3,000 a year, and the solar radiation in Lhasa tops the country because of minimal loss of sunshine when going through the atmosphere thanks to the high altitude and clean air. The sky over Lhasa is frequently blue with patches of white clouds, so Lhasa has earned the name of "city of sunshine."

In recent years people of Lhasa have intensified the use of renewable solar energy in the form of greenhouses, solar stoves for heating water and houses, with better day lighting and thermal insulation, in an effort to conserve firewood, coal and other bio-fuels and fossil fuels, which are in short supply locally, and reduce air pollution.

V. Yamzho Yumco — A Pearl in Southern Tibet

A broad bend of the Yarlung Zangbo not far from the Quxu Bridge is a habitat for black-necked cranes in winter. As many as 100 or more cranes can be seen perching on the sandbanks in this section of the river, which is quite secluded. Listed as a first-class nationally protected species, this migratory bird has habitats in many lakes and swamps on the Qinghai-Tibet Plateau, like the Zoige Marshes in western Sichuan, Nagpag Co in Yunnan, Ga Hai Lake in Qinghai, Xainza in Nagqu Prefecture, and Ngari Prefecture. When winter approaches, they migrate to relatively warmer valleys on the middle reaches of the Yarlung Zangbo to spend the winter and return to their original habitats in northern Tibet and other places the following spring. The black-necked crane, native to the Qinghai-Tibet Plateau, is all the more rare because of its low breeding rate. Tibetans have always taken good care of them, regarding them as holy birds since ancient times. In recent years, a nature reserve has been set up in Xainza, its breeding ground in northern Tibet. Appropriate protective measures are under study to protect the ecological environment of its over-wintering ground on the middle reaches of Yarlung Zangbo.

Shortly after this, a hairpin road leads to the Damba Pass, 5,000 m above sea level. Although not particularly high, the pass serves as the watershed dividing the exorheic Yarlung Zangbo and the inland water systems of southern Tibet, including Yamzho Yumco. Standing on the pass dotted with cairns called "mani", which are decorated with colourful sutra streamers fluttering in the winds, one can have a bird's eye view of Yamzho Yumco at the foot of the mountain. This is the largest inland lake in southern Tibet. It is irregularly shaped, like a river meandering through high mountains, now widening up and now narrowing down, with numerous bays and islets. An aerial view

A "pearl" on the southern Tibetan plateau — Yamzho Yumco.

profiles it like a swan in flight. It is 20-40 m deep, and the water is so clear that the luxuriant waterweeds in shallower places can clearly be seen swaying gently under water, with fish swimming in their midst. The lake abounds in highland scale-less carp, a common variety in highland lakes. Except for the anal scales and a few irregular scales remaining at the shoulder, those on its body have degenerated so that the fish is virtually naked. Local fishermen use big wooden boats to catch these fish, and their catches are sizeable, so the lake is referred to as Tibet's "fish store." A little farther into the lake, groups of reddy shelducks, brown-headed gulls and other birds can be seen swimming playfully.

A Lamasery of the Nyingma (Red) Sect stands on a larger islet in the lake. Rising smoke from burning incense, the chiming of bells and the beating of drums add to the lake a mysterious touch. The snow-capped Mount Nyingjinkangsha (7,206 m above sea level) to the west is reflected in the lake.

Yamzho Yumco is held in esteem as a "holy lake" by the local people. It is the fifth-largest in Tibet, and one of the four well-known "yumco's" (the other three being neighboring Puma Yumco, Ngari's Mapam Yumco and northern Tibet's Tangra Yumco). In the Tibetan language, "yumco" means a "jade lake," and "yamzho" means an "upper pasture." From its name it can be seen that Yamzho Yumco is known far and wide for its clean water, while the vast pastures around the lake, at least half a million ha in area, are a famous grazing ground in Tibet.

Surrounded by high mountains and replenished by melted snow and ice and rainfall, Yamzho Yumco is brackish, and covers an area of 649 sq km. As for its origin, some specialists hold that it is a structural lake as a result of depression in the course of the plateau's uplifting, while others theorize that it used to be an exorheic lake that had flown into Yarlung Zangbo through Manqu near Baidi on the northwest edge of the lake but was later cut off from the river to become a landlocked one, because the passage linking the two was blocked by torrential sediments as the climate became drier. The water of the lake was also mineralized to some extent. Moreover, some smaller lakes are found in its vicinity, such as Cheng Co, Kongmu Co and Bajiu Co, all of which used to be part of the larger Yamzho Yumco. They were disconnected from one another because of the blocking of the nearby rivers by sediment and a drop in the water level.

Yamzho Yumco and the Yarlung Zangbo, located on opposite sides of the Kamba watershed, are only eight km apart, but show a great difference in height, with the lake's water surface more than 800 m higher than that of the river. A tunnel through Mount Kamba to lead water from the lake to the river will make it possible to generate electricity by making use of the high headwater, and ease the power shortage in the Lhasa area. The construction of the Yamzho Yumco Hydroelectric Power Station was started in 1989, and it went into trial operation in June 1997. With an installed generating capacity of 112.5 kw, it is a medium-sized storage hydroelectric power station with the highest altitude, the greatest headwater and the longest tunnel in China at present. Its completion will greatly speed up the economic development of the area of "one river plus two tributaries," improve the living and production conditions of the local people, and benefit the ecological environment of the Yarlung Zangbo valley.

VI. The "Heroic City" (Gyangze) and the Best Plantation (Xigaze)

Leaving Yamzho Yumco, passing through the seat of Nagarze County and continuing in a westward direction, one will soon get to the pass on Mount Karala. Not far from the pass and on the right of the Sino-Nepalese Highway is the tip of a glacier (4,900 m above sea level). One can see the mist rising from the ice surface and feel the chilling cold without leaving one's vehicle. Or one may walk a short distance to take a closer look at the glacier since it is the one closest to a highway in Tibet.

After leaving the Karala Pass, one enters the valley of the Nyangqu River, the largest tributary on the southern bank of the Yarlung Zangbo. Some 216.3 km long, it drains an area of 11,100 sq km, close to one third of the Lhasa River valley. It ranks fifth among the tributaries of the Yarlung Zangbo in terms of length and drainage size.

As the Nyangqu River flows in a northwest direction generally at an altitude of 4,000 m, it decreases in elevation, and its valley keeps widening, until it becomes 3-5 km wide at Gyangze. As is the case with the Lhasa River, the strath of Nyangqu River is also a "granary" of Tibet and a key area for agricultural production in the area of "one river plus two tributaries." In this part of Tibet are located Tibet's second-largest city, Xigaze, and the famous city of Gyangze, with its glorious history.

The first thing a visitor to Gyangze sees is a rocky peak rising abruptly from the plain and a fortress on its lofty top, which is the famed Dzong Hill. In 1904, the local people held this fortress for more than three months in a heroic struggle against British invaders, and more than 200 of them died in the battle there. Gyangze has thus won the name "heroic city." The State Council has listed it as a famous historical and cultural city, and the fortress and the gun batteries on the hill used in the anti-British battle as major cultural relics under state protection.

Gyangze carpets (local name *"kadian"*) are famous Tibetan handicraft products, dating back more than 600 years. Woven tightly with a unique

Livestock at pasture in southern Tibet, with Mount Everest (Qomolangma) in the distance.

technique, they are of fine workmanship, durable and gorgeous. Their designs have figures of dragons, deer, phoenixes and butterflies, as well as landscapes and plants, in a rich Tibetan style. They are famous both in China and abroad. Many foreign visitors can be seen buying locally produced carpets in stores here. Gyangze carpets are made of wool from the Tibetan sheep native to the plateau. Such wool, although somewhat coarse in texture, is elastic and lustrous, and most suitable for carpet making, hence the sheep are called "carpet sheep." Commercial production bases of "carpet sheep" have been set up in northern Tibetan pastures to meet the needs of Tibetan carpet production.

Xigaze, Tibet's second-largest city, lies 86 km north of Gyangze and at an altitude of 3,800 m. The road linking the two cities goes through the broad valley of the Nyangqu River, whose shallow bed often branches off into four or five prongs to form a mesh-like water system, with numerous sandbanks, while there are quite a few aeolian dunes and sandy slopes on the eastern bank of the river. The Nyangqu and Lhasa river valleys share basically the same natural features, although the Nyangqu has a smaller flow and its soil is drier, with quite a few places suffering from a shortage of water. The Gyangze-Xigaze area is a key area for farmland irrigation in the agricultural development project of the area of "one river plus two tributaries." In the Tibetan language, "Xigaze" means a "plantation of the best soil," because the land there is quite fertile. The city has a history of more than 600 years. It is said to have grown out of a group of temples, hence its old name "Tashilhunpo." It used to be the official residence of the Panchen Erdenis, and the political and religious center of Tsang (western Tibet). It attracts a steady flow of tourists every year, thanks to the famous Tashilhunpo Monastery in the city and Mount Qomolangma not far away. The open Xigaze is becoming ever more attractive to the outside world, and is a must-see city for visitors, like Lhasa.

The impressive Tashilhunpo Monastery at the foot of Mount Nyima is second only to the Potala in scale. In front of the gate pilgrims perform their religious rituals, and there are stalls selling daily necessities, arts and crafts, and religious articles, as well as restaurants and teahouses.

Xigaze is a Buddhist holy place, with many sites of historical interest. On its outskirts lies another of Tibet's grain production centers. Enjoying ample sunshine and solar radiation, and given better irrigation and field management, a good harvest of 400-500 kg *qingke* per *mu* is often reaped and in some cases even a harvest of 900 kg per *mu* has been reported. It is one of the high-yield wheat producers in Tibet, and it is expected that after the project of the "one river plus two tributaries" is completed, agricultural production there will reach a new level, making Xigaze an important "granary" for Tibet.

VII. The Green Treasure House — the Nyang River Area

After leaving Nang Xian Gorge, the Yarlung Zangbo valley begins to spread slightly and the river flows on for more than 20 km before entering the 10-km-long Rimin Gorge. The 170-km-long wide valley between the Rimin Gorge and Paixiang, which lies at an altitude of 2,800 m, is the last section of the wide valley on the middle reaches of the Yarlung Zangbo. The water surface in this section is two km at the widest, and the valley floor is more than three km wide where it is joined by the Nyang River. The Yarlung Zangbo in this section flows slowly, and there are a fair number of shoals, prongs and sandbanks in the river course, as well as crescent-shaped sand dunes on both banks, but not as many or as large as in the Zetang section.

The Nyang River is 286 km long and covers a drainage area of 17,500 sq km, ranking fourth among the numerous tributaries of Yarlung Zangbo. But it ranks second in terms of flow, only after the Parlung Zangbo. That is because there are developed maritime glaciers as a result of extensive high peaks in the valley and prevailing humid air currents from the Indian Ocean. The marked increase in atmospheric precipitation (about 650 mm annually in this area) and a large amount of melted snow and ice provide plentiful replenishments for the Nyang River, with its annual runoff reaching 22 billion cu m. Thanks to the extensive forest cover

A view of the Nyang River near Nyingchi.

and the 34-percent vegetation coverage, the Nyang River contains only a small amount of silt, even in the summer flood season. Its clear water reflects the heavily forested mountains on both banks and the snow-capped peaks under the blue sky. The climate in the Nyang River valley is mild and pleasant, with an average annual temperature of 8.6 degrees centigrade and the highest temperature hitting 30.2 degrees centigrade in summer. The rainfall is moderate. The altitude of the valley is not high, ranging between 2,900 m and 4,000 m. There are large tracts of farmland on both banks, especially at the river mouth, which are suitable for growing not only *qingke* and wheat, but also apple, walnut and other fruit trees of economic value. Its rich forest reserves have turned it into a timber producer for Tibet, and it is an important part of China's southwest forest area. Among the valuable forest products are musk, glossy ganoderma (*Ganoderma lucidum*) and pine mushrooms. The local musk has been singled out as "western musk" for its superior quality, big size, thin shell, full kernel and strong fragrance. The kernel, in particular, is considered to yield the best musk. Musk is used not only in perfumery, but also as an excitant and stimulant in medicine. Pine mushrooms are prized as edible fungus and for their anti-carcinogenic quality. They have been exported to Japan in large quantities in recent years. In addition, there is a great

variety of animals on the list of state-pro-
tected species, first- and second-class,
such as Tibetan eared pheasant, crimson-
bellied tragopan and white-bellied
pheasant, as well as beautifully plumaged
birds of ornamental value, such as the red-
billed leiothrix, sunbird and songbird. Diversified bio-resources are a valuable
natural asset of the Nyang River valley.
The forests, in particular, are not only its
dominant resource, promising broad prospects for development, but also a natural
green biological barrier on the plateau that
plays an important role in conserving

Red-billed leiothrix.

water, regulating the climate and protecting the environment of the eastern
Tibetan mountains. In addition, the area is ideal for developing tourism and
holiday resorts. All this makes the Nyang River a green treasure house with
very broad prospects for development in the Yarlung Zangbo valley.

A golden pheasant. The male is famed for its
gorgeous plumage.

Bayi (August 1) Town,
the seat of the Nyingchi
prefectural government,
is located on a terrace, 1-
2 m high, on the right
bank of the Nyang River,
at an altitude of approximately 3,000 m above
sea level. It had been a
wilderness haunted by
wild animals before a

woolen textile mill was moved there from Shanghai to become the first light industrial enterprise in Tibet, in 1966. Thanks to construction over the decades since then, the town now boasts close to 100 industrial enterprises and institutions. Apart from the renowned Nyingchi Woolen Textile Mill, there are the Tibet Matches Mill and Tibet Agro-Animal Husbandry College, as well as a printing house, power-generating plants, wood-processing mills and other industrial installations that source their raw materials locally. Rows of buildings and private dwellings line the river. Since it was built with the joint efforts of local civilians and soldiers of the People's Liberation Army, this new town on the Nyang River was named "Bayi" (August 1, the Army Day) in recognition of the PLA's contribution.

Bayi Town is the political, economic and cultural center of Nyingchi Prefecture, in eastern Tibet. Its woolen blankets are exported all over the world, its forest, sideline, native and special products enjoy a high reputation among consumers, and it has trained many Tibetan agronomists and animal husbandry specialists. It is also an important hub on the Sichuan-Tibet Highway. As travelers going from Sichuan to Tibet must go through this place, shops, inns, and other catering and recreational facilities have boomed in the town. Benbo Hill, to the south of the town, although not high, is a holy place according to the ancient Tibetan Bon religion. Every April by the Tibetan calendar, Bon followers make rounds of the hill in a religious ritual. This hill is covered with heavy trees and grass, and has a supposedly sacred spring, the water of which is believed to help prolong life. Numerous sutra streamers of all colors and white *hada* (ceremonial scarves) trail from tree branches and Mani piles around the well.

Bangna Village, east of the hill, boasts a 1,300-year-old mulberry tree, rarely seen elsewhere in the country. Said to have been planted at the time of the marriage of Princess Wencheng and Songtsen Gampo, this tree is seven m

A vulture.

tall and 3.3 m in diameter.

In neighboring Bajie Village a nature reserve covering only eight ha was established in 1985 to protect ancient cypresses. These trees average 50 m in height and one m in diameter. The biggest one is at least 2,500 years old. It has a diameter of six m and takes about ten people to encircle it with their arms. With the Latin name *cypressus gigantea Cheng et L. K. Fu*, and also known as Yarlung Zangbo cypress, it is native to Tibet and listed among the second-class nationally protected plants. It is a "living fossil," as its trunk records ecological and environmental changes in this highland region over the past 1,000 years.

An orchard near the county seat boasts a great variety of fruit trees, such as apple, peach, pear and walnut, local or introduced from elsewhere. The Nyang River valley is particularly suitable for growing these fruits. The local apples are of fine quality, and their output ranks first in Tibet. Walnut trees are seen everywhere, in front of every home, on the edge of every village, and along roads and trails. There are ten varieties of walnut, all of fine quality, notably the "butter walnut," which is large and has a thin shell, and the "exposed-kernel walnut," the kernel of which is partially exposed. So apple and walnut will be the focus of fruit tree development in the Nyang River valley in the future, and the dominant fruit products of Nyingchi Prefecture.

Some 140 km from Bayi Town is Conggo Co (also known as Basong Lake), lying 3,538 m above sea level. Covering an area of 26 sq km, it is an alpine lake on the upper reaches of the Bahe River. It is a drift barrier lake created during the heyday of the Quaternary glaciation, when the terminal welts left by the former glaciers of the Nyainqentanglha Mountains blocked the valley of the Bahe River. With a maximum depth of 60 m, the lake water is clear and blue. Around the lake are heavily forested mountains, with peaks thrusting into the sky and the snow on their tops glistening in the sun. Such a natural scenery of lakes and mountains reminds people of Switzerland. An islet in the lake is a giant embossed rock left by an ancient glacier. On the islet is a 17th-century Lamasery of the Gelug school (Yellow Sect) of Tibetan Buddhism. Beside the lamasery is a bizarre tree — a walnut tree parasitic on a pine tree. This two-in-one tree and what are said to be the prints of hooves left by the horse of the legendary Tibetan hero, King Gesar, are tourist attractions on the islet, which is accessible by special rafts for tourists.

Basum Co (Lake Conggo) is one of Tibet's most popular tourist areas.

Conggo Co promises to become the most attractive tourist site in the Nyang River valley.

VIII. The Himalayan Geothermal Belt

The Tibet plateau tops China in the number and types of geothermal fields, hot springs and mineral springs, and in the grandeur of their spectacles, and may even be listed among the famous hot springs worldwide. There are, all together, 31 large geyser zones worldwide and Tibet is one of them. Yangbajain Geothermal Field is the largest one of its kind in Tibet, and probably in China as well. There are 660 geothermal manifestations in Tibet, including hydrothermal explosions, geysers, boiling springs, hot springs, thermal springs, pools of boiling mud, steaming zones and sinters. They are distributed along the Great Sengge Zangbo (Shiquan River)-Yarlung Zangbo Fracture Belt, known as the Himalayan Geothermal Belt. Lying mainly between the Himalayas and the Gangdise Mountains, it extends 2,000 km at an average altitude of 4,000 m, and is linked with the Mediterranean Geothermal Belt to the west and the Pacific Geothermal Belt to the east and south, forming a very important part of the geothermal belt in the world.

The Himalayan Geothermal Belt displays hydrothermal activity with an intensity equal to that of recent or modern volcanic areas. Hydrothermal explosions and geysers which had been thought to be exclusive to volcanic areas are to be found on the Tibetan plateau. So far, a dozen hydrothermal explosions and four geyser zones have been discovered in Tibet, with an intensity and frequency of activity rarely seen elsewhere in the world. For example, on November 12, 1975, a particularly big hydrothermal explosion occurred in a village close to the Sino-Nepalese border, the largest ever recorded in China. At the time of the explosion, a giant dark-grey smoke column was sent 800 m to 900 m into the air, and a rock with the diameter of a large pan near the crater was tossed up and landed one km away. A 25-m crater was created, which now has turned into a hydrothermal lake. The Tagejia Geyser Zone in Ngamring County on the Yarlung Zangbo, at an altitude of 5,030 m above sea level, is the highest of its kind in the world. Its main spring's activity is not regular, but when in full display, its water-steam column, about two m in diameter, can reach a height of 20 m. It is the

A geothermal manifestation.

largest geyser in China, and indeed in Asia. Geothermal manifestations of different types are distributed all over the Himalayan Geothermal Zone. Their strong hydrothermal activity and the nearby snow-capped peaks are the wonders on the "roof of the world."

The numerous hot springs in Tibet often have therapeutic and health-care effects, which have been recorded in many history books and medical literature. They have also constituted a subject of poetry. Among the better-known spas are Xungbalaqu Hot Spring in Doilungdeqen County, Kangbugou Hot Spring in Yadong County, Xiqin Hot Spring in Lhaze County, Milashan Hot Spring in Gongbo'gyamda County and Oiga Hot Spring in Qusum County. They have therapeutic effects on bone fractures, kidney inflammation, skin diseases, eye diseases, and digestive and cardio-vascular diseases. In addition, Tibet is an area with the greatest concentration of the least polluted mineral water in China. More than 630 mineral springs have been verified, representing the greatest number in China. Much of the mineral water of fine quality contains a good variety of trace elements, which are good for the health and have proved effective for the treatment of some diseases. Mineral water in commercial production includes Qudengnyima Holy Water and Himalayan Mineral Water. Sweetish and refreshing, they have been marketed in a dozen countries and regions.

IX. The World's No. 1 Great Canyon

The Great Canyon of the Yarlung Zangbo extends 504.6 km from the Paiqu section in Mainling County, passing the southeast side of Mount Namjagbarwa and to its exit at Baxika. The most dangerously steep section is between Daduka in Paiqu and Bangbo in Medog County, 240 km long and with an average depth of 5,000 m. The deepest point, at 5,382 m, is between Mount

The Great Canyon of the Yarlung Zangbo.

Namjagbarwa and Mount Jialabailei, where the riverbed is more than 200 m at the widest and only 35 m at the narrowest. The longitudinal section of the entire Great Canyon is an asymmetrical V-shape, with the face of the slopes being slightly inflected into a terrace shape, wide at the upper part and steep and narrow at the lower part, which in many places presents a U-shape. The rocky walls of the valley are more than 300 m above the water surface and on both sides are precipitous monoclinal mountains featuring cliffs and forbidding peaks. Many small bends are telescoped, and the gorge looks magnificent like an incised meander with a staggering of inset basal beds and prongs. The Great Canyon of the Yarlung Zangbo is the biggest gorge in the world in terms of length and depth, as well as altitude in the world.

The Great Canyon is the largest and the most important passage on the Tibet plateau for the warm and humid air currents from the Indian Ocean, resulting in many peculiar biological and geological features, and rich natural resources all the way along the passage. Along the gorge, the tropical limits can be extended northward by as many as five parallels to become the northernmost limits of the tropical zone on the northern hemisphere. Therefore, the Great Canyon has become an area with the richest biological realms on the entire Qinghai-Tibet Plateau, including two-thirds of the known higher plants, half of the known mammals and four-fifths of the known insects on the plateau, as well as three-fifths of the known large fungi in China. It has immense potential for hydropower, with two-thirds of the total hydropower resources of the Yarlung Zangbo concentrated there, and the greatest hydropower reserve per unit area among the world's larger rivers of the same kind. According to calculations, its maximum natural hydropower reserve exceeds 68,800 mw, averaging 138.6 mw per km. Mount Namjagbarwa, on the southern flank of the Great Canyon, is one of the centers of violent uplifting of the Himalayas, while the Great Bend, which accommodates the multi-directional, complex structural development, is where the structure is inflected and the stress

The Yarlung Zangbo Grand Canyon is the largest water channel between
the Indian Ocean and the Qinghai-Tibet Plateau.

focussed. The modern tectonic movement, as represented by earthquakes, is
violent and frequent, constantly changing the topography of the Great Canyon,
so that a good number of high-heat geothermal manifestations have emerged.

A number of microlithic sites have been discovered in longshore terraces
along the valley of the Great Canyon. The unearthed articles are similar to
those unearthed on the northern flank of the Himalayas. This shows that as
far back as 5,000-8,000 years ago people lived in and travelled through this
area, which has played an important role in contacts between lowland and
highland ethnic groups. Even today, thousands of Moinbas, Luobas and Tibetans still live in this harsh and remote region. They have kept intact the
languages, costumes, religious beliefs and the ages-old customs and habits
of their own ethnic groups, such as totem worship and belief in deities and

ghosts, sorcery, divination by killing cocks and cattle as sacrifices. Such customs and habits handed down from the time of the primitive tribes are part of the cultural and historical heritage shared by mankind the world over and "living fossils" for ethnological studies.

The Great Canyon has caught the attention of the world for its exceptional grandeur and special features. With the establishment of national forest parks in the Great Canyon and its surrounding area (Paiqu and Parlung, for example), improvement of roads and establishment of necessary tourism facilities, this world-class gorge will in time become a world-famous tourist site.

In 1998, a joint expedition sent by the Chinese Academy of Sciences surveyed the uninhabited section that forms the core of the Great Canyon (a 20-odd-km section from Ximila to Za Qu, where the Parlung Zangbo meets the Yarlung Zangbo). It discovered groups of riverbed waterfalls that are rarely seen elsewhere in the world. This section of the gorge has many bends, and the riverbed is particularly steep, with an average gradient of 23 per thousand. Field surveys show that the narrowest point of the river trough set into the basal bed is only 35 m, and there is a 21-m difference between the high and low waters. The team confirmed or discovered four groups of waterfalls.

The name of Mount Namjagbarwa, inside the horseshoe-shaped Great Bend, means "a spear that pierces the sky" in the Tibetan language. It is 7,782 m above sea level and, although ranking only 15th in the world in terms of height, it is well known worldwide for its capricious weather and complex and dangerous mountain structure. The peak is almost always shrouded by clouds. It is located at a pivotal position between the giant Himalayas and the bend of the Yarlung Zangbo, and its shape, water system, geological structure, and animals and plants all show a unique transitional feature. In terms of geological structure, it is at the northeast tip of the Indian Plate that dives at

The riverbed of the Great Canyon of the Yarlung Zangbo is full of twists and turns, with the riverbed cut into the basal rock.

the Eurasian Plate, and a transitional belt where different structures converge, recombine and hinge. It is an ideal place for studying the features of the crustal structures of the Himalayas and of the mechanism of plate movement. Apart from fairly rich hot spring resources, it also shows a distinct, complex and fairly complete altitudinal spectrum of mountain plants. For example, there are five altitudinal belts on its northern slope, but as many as nine on the southeast slope, which is rare elsewhere in the country.

This peak is a well-known holy mountain in southeast Tibet. Legend has it that once upon a time there were two brothers, named Namjagbarwa and Jialabailei, who had been sent by God to guard southeast Tibet. Jialabailei, the younger brother, was diligent and keen to learn, so he grew taller and taller every day, while his combat skills kept improving. Out of jealousy, Namjagbarwa, the elder brother, cut off the head of his younger brother when the latter was sound asleep. From then on, the younger brother stopped growing, and turned into a headless mountain. Mount Dela, near Mainling, is said to have evolved from his severed head. Namjagbarwa, on the other hand, was ordered to guard the river all his life as a punishment for his crime.

Medog County lying in the depth of the Great Canyon is a beautiful "isolated island" virtually cut off from the outside world. According to a legend, Dorjepam created this sacred place out of his own body. It is supposed to be the "land of the pure" and a "Buddhist paradise." For centuries, many Moinba, Luoba and Tibetan people have left their homes and travelled along the Yarlung Zangbo valley in search of this sacred place. They finally settled down in mountain-girt Paimakang (an old name for Medog).

Medog means "flower" in Tibetan. It is said that a girl named Meiduo (meaning "beautiful flower") came from far away to settle here. She was sincere, kind-hearted and hospitable. She treated whoever came with butter tea and wine. Everybody aspired to have a sip of her butter tea. Since her name was on everybody's lips, the place came to be known as Medog. The local Moinba and Luoba people follow the ages-old tradition of rising at sunrise and retiring at sunset, hunting or practicing slash-and-burn cultivation. They live a primitive life in isolation from modern civilisation. Therefore, the cultural landscape is very special, simple, natural and fascinating.

The Great Canyon is deep and dangerously steep, and the trails leading into it are extremely difficult. Anyone who wishes to explore has to walk from its periphery to Medog, and then into the canyon. Blocked by Mount Namjagbarwa and other high mountains and isolated by the Great Canyon, Medog is the only county in China that is not accessible by road. The steep, fragmented terrain, and violent and frequent avalanches, landfalls and landslides make it hard to build or maintain a road. Medog is snowbound and totally cut off from the interior of the plateau for eight to nine months a year. Explorers can go into the canyon between July and October, when the snow melts. There are six routes leading into the canyon.

Six

THE GROTESQUE MOUN-
TAINS AND GORGES OF
SOUTHEAST TIBET

A Sketch Map of the Three-river Drainage Area in Eastern Tibet

The mountain area of southeast Tibet embraces most of Qamdo and Nyingchi prefectures. There are great ups and downs in this area, and the mountains are rugged and complex. It is the western part of China's well-known Hengduan Mountains. The mountains are high and the gorges deep, the altitudinal changes in the ecological and climatic environments are conspicuous,

A Douglas fir.

Broom-handle fungus and other epiphytic plants in the mixed needle and broadleaf forests in the Hengduan Mountains.

with lush alpine pastures and virgin forests, and a great variety of animals and plants. It is the area of Tibet with the best bio-climatic conditions and most varied geographical landscapes. This area features the Yulong Copper Field, with the largest reserve of copper in the country, and the immense hydropower potential of the Jinsha, Lancang and Nujiang rivers as well as the Parlung Zangbo. The large-scale maritime glaciers in the southern section of the Nyainqentanglha Mountains and the eastern section of the Himalayas are a "solid-state reservoir" which replenishes the rivers and lakes within the area. The numerous valley glaciers are a special sight. This area boasts a denser population and its economy is relatively more developed than in other parts of Tibet, thanks to busier cultural and commercial exchanges between Tibetan and Han people on account of its proximity to Han-inhabited Chengdu, capital of Sichuan Province.

I. The Ancient Town of Qamdo — Gateway of Eastern Tibet

Qamdo Prefecture has an area of 108,900 sq km, accounting for nine percent of the total area of the Tibet Autonomous Region. Its capital, Qamdo Town, is situated at the confluence of the Za Qu and Ngom Qu rivers on the upper reaches of the Lancang River and at an altitude of 3,200 m above sea level. The valley is not extensive, and the houses are mostly built along the rivers and against mountains, with the old ones mixed with the new. Although a bit crowded, the town leaves visitors with a welcome impression of mysterious antiquity.

Qamdo has always been an important town in Eastern Tibet, a gateway guarding the entrance to Tibet from Sichuan, Yunnan and Qinghai provinces. It is the hub of transport in Eastern Tibet as the Sichuan-Tibet and Yunnan-Tibet Highways run through it. As the seat of the prefectural government, it is the political, economic, and cultural and communications center of Eastern Tibet. Its urban area is five sq km, and its population, over 7,000.

Thanks to its advantageous geographical position, Qamdo has long played an important role in facilitating the cultural and economic exchanges between Tibet and the interior part of China. It occupied a strategic position on the famous ancient "tea-for-horses" trading route. As a city with a long history and highly developed culture, it offers rich and colorful attractions to visitors. Stone and pottery articles, and ruins of ancient earthen walls, have been excavated in Karo Village, 12 km south to the town, in recent years, attesting to the fact that it was a site of human settlement in the Neolithic Age, 4,000-5,000 years ago. It is one of the three hitherto known primitive cultural sites in Tibet. Ancient grains of millet and bones of domestic pigs excavated from these sites are proof that the people of that time were already engaged in agriculture and livestock breeding.

There are some 25 holy mountains in the Qamdo area, the most famous of which is Mount Deqenpozhang in Riwoqe, which, though not very high, is picturesque and charming. Mount Gubu in Qamdo is high and steep, and riddled with caves, as it is comprised of limestone. Mount Dolha, in Baima Town, Baxoi County, contains hundreds of images of the Buddha carved on rocks, which are also inscribed with mantras. There are also the Caiwarong, Boren and Langkaze holy mountains in the Zogang-Baxoi area. Mount Sengqenlangza in Gamtog, Jomda County, is the most important of the holy mountains in the Qamdo area. It was where Master Padma-sambhava and venerable monks of the Nyingmapa (Old Order) and the Kagyurpa (the Order of the Transmitted Word) cultivated themselves in Buddhism. Every year, on the 15th day of the sixth month by the Tibetan calendar, devout Buddhists in their holiday best go to pay homage to the holy mountain, carrying food and *qingke* wine, and reciting mantras. They coat the Buddha images on the rocks with butter as they make ritualistic circuits of the mountain.

Mount Zedrup, in Dengqen County, is sacred to the followers of Bon, the native Tibetan religion.

There are also quite a few holy lakes in Qamdo Prefecture, the most famous of which is Lake Rawu, in Baxoi County. There are also Mang Co, in Markam County, the "Three Colors in One-Pool" Lake, in Banbar County, and the "21 Taras" Lake in Lhorong County.

Among hot springs with therapeutic effects in this area, too, are Yiri Hot Spring in Riwoqe, which is recommended for the treatment of rheumatism, arthritis, infantile calcium deficiency and skin diseases; Wameika Hot Spring in Qamdo; and 108 hot springs in Quzika, Yanjing Township.

Qamdo Town is the third most important town in Tibet, after Lhasa and Xigaze, on account of its long history and adjacency to the interior part of China. Qamdo Prefecture is the most densely populated area in Tibet, averaging five persons per sq km, as against 1.9 persons per sq km for the autonomous region as a whole. It used to be part of China's old Xikang Province. Therefore, the Tibetans living there are called "Kangpos," and the local culture is called "Kangpo Culture".

The ancient town of Qamdo has experienced great changes since the 1950s. When a visitor crosses the concrete bridge over the Lancang River to the old town, he or she will find the streets filled with rows of shops. Qamdo also boasts the tallest building in Tibet, at ten stories. In contrast to this modern

A subnival meadow grazing ground at the foot of Mount Dagmala.

An ancient karst land feature.

touch of the town are stalls selling all kinds of Tibetan arts and crafts, such as rosaries, bronze statues of the Buddha and other religious articles, bracelets, necklaces, carpets, Tibetan knives and daily necessities. Monks in maroon robes can be seen mingling with the crowds in the meandering lanes, where gold, silver and copper smiths ply their trades.

Mount Dagmala (meaning "azalea" in Tibetan), lying near the town on the eastern side of the Lancang River is the last high mountain on the route from Sichuan to Tibet. Although it is not particularly high (about 5,000 m above sea level), it is quite impressive. It is named after the azalea flowers which bloom in May and June each year. Some flowers have a diameter of a large bowl or a cup, while others are as small as bean sprouts, in white, pink, yellow or purple.

Travelers on the highway that skirts the mountain will also see a kind of special landform, notably jagged rocky walls extending along some mountain ridges like a set of dog's fangs or the vertebrae of a fish. This is due to erosion by the wet and warm climate during the Tertiary period or even earlier, some one million years ago, of the limestone strata that form the mountains, in the same way as the karst features emerged in inland China's Guangxi Zhuang Autonomous Region and Guizhou Province. Although the rocky walls were subsequently raised to an altitude of 4,500 m above sea level as a result of a violent neotectonic movement and were exposed to long-time weathering, they have remained fairly well preserved as a site of ancient karst features rare elsewhere in Tibet. Today, people can still see clearly such vestiges of the ancient karst features as caves and holes in the steep cliffs, and clints and "stone forests" on the ridges surrounding the rocky walls. Mount Zhujiao, 40 km from Qamdo Town, is a summer resort with picturesque scenery and a pleasant climate. Here, in 1992, Chinese and German scientists discovered a forest of cypresses, dating back to the Tang Dynasty and estimated to be about 1,300 years old.

Qamdo Prefecture is rich in natural resources. The Yulong porphyry copper mine in Jomda County, less than 200 km east of Qamdo is among the largest high-grade copper fields in China, with an initial verified reserve of 6.5 million tons, with sizable reserves of coexisting iron, silver and molybdenum. At an altitude of about 5,000 m above sea level, the mine is the world's highest copper producer.

The extensive forests in the Qamdo area offer a rich variety of products, such as apples, pears and peaches in Chagyab and Baxoi counties, as well as walnuts, grapes and pomegranates elsewhere. The area is also famous for its wide variety of edible mushrooms. In addition to the common types, there are more valuable types, including hedgehog hudnum, pine mushrooms, scaly tooth and morels, which enjoy fame at home and abroad. The pine mushroom, in particular, shows an especially strong anti-mutation ability, which enabled it to become the only plant to survive the nuclear radiation resulting from the atomic bomb explosion in Japan during the Second World War. Anti-carcinogenic drugs made of pine mushroom extract are popular in Japan and Southeast Asia while pine mushrooms as health food having anti-cancer effects also sell well in Japan. Pine mushrooms grow in large quantities in the forests of alpine oak, in southern Qamdo and the contiguous Baima Snow Mountains in northwest Yunnan Province. The July-September rainy season each

The Yunnan golden monkey is a rare animal under top state protection.

The lesser panda is under first-class state protection.

year is the picking season, when local people flock to the forests, and camp out there, picking mushrooms day and night. Trucks carry the fresh mushrooms to the nearby Zhongdian Airport for direct air shipment to Japan.

In addition, the Qamdo area boasts 1,200 kinds of medicinal herbs, of which musk, Chinese caterpillar fungus, bulb of fritillary, bezoar and snow lotus, as well as pilose antlers, are exported in large quantities and become an important source of income for the local people. There are more than 600 kinds of wild animals in the local forests and pastures. Among those listed as wildlife under state protection, first and second class, are Biet's monkey (Yunnan golden monkey), serow, sambar, Thorad's deer (white-lipped deer), Moschus berezovskii, lesser panda, white-bellied pheasant, Tibetan eared pheasant, and a number of other pheasants. Quite a few of them are native only to the Qinghai-Tibetan plateau. For example, Biet's monkey, one of the three subspecies native to China, is a rare animal referred to as China's "second national treasure" after the giant panda. There are four subspecies of golden monkeys — the Vietnamese golden monkey, and the Sichuan, Guizhou and Yunnan golden monkeys — that are native to China. They are also listed in the global data book of animals on the brink of extinction. The Yunnan golden monkey was identified for the first time by a French zoologist in

1897. There were no further reports of sightings of this animal until 1962, when eight hides of Yunnan golden monkeys were collected in Deqen, Yunnan, confirming the continued existence of this rare animal in the Hengduan Mountains. Surveys in recent years have revealed that there are about 1,000-1,500 Yunnan golden monkeys surviving, mainly distributed in the high, densely forested mountains in the adjoining areas of Tibet and Yunnan, including the Baima Snowy Mountains of Yunnan and the adjoining Mount Markam in Qamdo. Unlike the other three subspecies, which sport long golden and lustrous hair, Yunnan golden monkeys have long and thick dark brown hair. They prefer to live in sub-alpine dark coniferous belts at an altitude of 3,000-4,000 m above sea level and higher, with the shoots of needle-leaf trees and hanging moss on their branches as their main food. They also eat algae on the rocks and, in spring, bamboo shoots. They are interdependent with alpine spruces and firs and conifers; and due to their feeding habits they live only in high-altitude dark needle-leaf tree belts, so that they are the only subspecies of the family of golden monkeys that live in high mountains. According to historical records, Yunnan golden monkeys once also lived in the Yangtze River valley in ancient times but were later compelled by the changes in the environment and human activity to retreat to the high mountains between Tibet and Yunnan. Yunnan golden monkey is the most specialized subspecies among the family of golden monkeys and the only non-human primate that lives at such a high altitude.

During the 1960s and 1970s, the number of golden monkeys in the Mount Markam area of southern Qamdo was estimated at more than 2,000, but this number dropped to about 700 in the late 1980s, as a result of poaching. After the Mount Markam Nature Reserve was established in 1988, their number tended to stabilize, and those in the nature reserve number approximately 650-750 at present, and are distributed in an insular pattern. Inside the nature reserve are also quite a few varieties of beautifully plumed pheasants, such as Tibetan snow cock, blood pheasant, crimson-bellied tragopan, Tibetan eared pheasant and golden pheasant. It is one of the areas in China with the richest varieties of pheasants. Some people claim that the Hengduan Mountains area, which encompasses Qamdo, is one of the world's biological differentiation centers, preserving many primitive bio-species. This has probably resulted from the mountain terrain here, which runs in a north-south direction. The unique geographical environment is a corridor for the meeting of different biological realms from the south and north and also a favorable place, or sanctuary, for the survival of many rare animals. For example, giant pandas, the sole species left over from the Tertiary Period, lives on in the Hengduan Mountains.

II. Three Rivers Running in Parallel

Qamdo Prefecture is situated on an inclined plane, a transitional zone from the Qinghai-Tibet Plateau towards its southeast peripheral areas (the Sichuan Basin and the Central Yunnan Highlands), with its northwestern part higher than the southeastern part. In terms of geological foundation, it belongs to an arc-shaped structural belt of three rivers. In the late Cretaceous Period, about 100 million years ago, what is now the Qamdo area detached itself entirely from the Tethys Sea, and rose to become a landmass. Subsequently it went through a number of tectonic uplifting movements, resulting in a series of folds and fracture belts running in a general direction from the northwest to southeast, with the folds becoming mountains, and the fractures, valleys. This basically shaped the unique terrain of the area featuring the alternation of ridges with valleys and their north-south formation. Especially over the most recent two to three million years, during the late Tertiary and the Quaternary periods, the violent neotectonic movements, and water erosion and scission have further sharpened the height difference between the ridges and valleys, resulting in the "transactional terrain" characterized by dangerously steep mountains and deep valleys, and making the area part of the famous Hengduan Mountains.

In the Qamdo area, the high mountain ranges alternating with the Jinsha, Lancang and Nujiang rivers in the tectonic fracture belt and running in a north-south direction are, from east to west, the Markam (Ningjing) range, the Taniantaweng range, the southern section of the Nyainqentanglha Mountains and the Baxoila Ridge. They are mostly at an altitude of 4,500-5,500 m above sea level, with many peaks exceeding 6,000 m. For example, the highest peak in the Nyainqentanglha Mountains is 6,956 m. Most of these high mountains have existing glaciers and present a magnificent view, with their tops covered by snow. The valleys of the three rivers, on the other hand, are 2,300-3,500 m above sea level, with the north higher than the south and a relative height difference of 2,000-2,500 m between the valleys and the mountains on both sides. Sandwiched between high, precipitous mountains, the valleys present a deep V shape in most cases, thus forming a virtually insurmountable natural barrier to east-west transportation between Tibet and Sichuan in the interior in view of the poor means of transportation in ancient times, hence the name "Hengduan (meaning traversal blocking) Mountains."

Mushrooms in an alpine meadow.

The reason why the Hengduan Mountains are famous in Chinese, and indeed world, geography is firstly their unique terrain, featuring the alternation of high mountain ranges with dangerously deep, big river valleys that run parallel to each other in a north-south direction; and secondly, a very peculiar geographical feature rarely seen in the world, that is, the great proximity between the three big rivers. For example, in the adjoining area between southeast Tibet and northwest Yunnan, that is, near the 28th Parallel N, the distance between the Jinsha and Lancang rivers and that between the Lancang and Nujiang rivers, as the crow flies, is only 53 km and 25 km, respectively. These three big Asian rivers flow torrentially side by side, southward, with so small a distance in between them — this is an exciting spectacle and a world-famous wonder. In addition, the area serves not only as the most wide-ranging museum of geology and topography in the world, it also boasts numerous diverse wild animals and plants and is a major north-south corridor and sanctuary for biospecies on the Eurasian continent. It has earned the name of "the world's bio-gene pool" for its rich and diversified bio-communities. Thanks to these universally acknowledged special features, the "Three Rivers Running in Parallel" were put on the "World Heritage List" by UNESCO'S World Heritage Committee in 2003, becoming China's fourth natural heritage site on the list (the other three being Jiuzhaigou, Huanglong and Wulingyuan).

The geological and geographical environments of the three rivers offer special, many-faceted natural beauty. If a traveler starts from Zhongdian in north-west Yunnan and travels upstream along the Lancang River by the Yunnan-Tibet Highway in a northward direction, he or she will see the charms of "Shangri-la", snow-capped Mount Moirig under blue skies with feathery clouds, the hot, dry and treeless valleys around Benzilan, expansive fertile farmland dotted with salt wells, and the pastoral scenes of the Bamda Grassland, where hordes of cattle and sheep graze. If he or she traverses the valleys of the three rivers along the Sichuan-Tibet Highway starting from Kangding and going westward, he or she will fully appreciate the hardships of travel in this rugged terrain. Of course, he or she will also be handsomely rewarded by an opportunity to experience the different climatic belts of the hot, dry farming areas in the valleys, pleasantly cool, tree-covered mountains and frozen alpine deserts strewn with gravel as the vehicle climbs mountains and glides along valleys. Unfolded are different natural features: fields, forests, alpine pastures and snow-capped peaks. Such phrases as "Ten *li* (half a km) means different climates" and "four seasons within the same mountain area" vividly describe the quick succession of natural scenes in the Hengduan Mountains of eastern Tibet.

This area receives an average annual precipitation of 400-600 mm. Replenished amply by melting snow, the rivers here have abundant water, with little seasonal fluctuation. The sections of the Jinsha, Lancang and Nujiang rivers within Qamdo Prefecture are 509 km, 509 km and 975 km in length, respectively, and their annual average volumes of flow are 238, 364 and 1,138 cu m per second respectively. Therefore, leaving aside the Jinsha River, which is the upstream of the Yangtze, China's longest river, the Nujiang and the Lancang are the second and third largest rivers in Tibet in terms of length and volume of flow after the Yarlung Zangbo. In addition, these rivers have steeply sloping beds, with the water drop exceeding 1,200 m and gradient topping two per thousand or even more than four per thousand at certain sections. The turbulent flow harbors an immensely abundant hydropower potential. The theoretical hydropower potential of the trunks of the three rivers alone totals 30,000 mw. Particularly, the sections of the three rivers and their numerous tributaries within the central and southern parts of the Qamdo area are mostly gorges, with little farmland and few hamlets, which are very suitable conditions for building high-dam reservoirs and staircase hydroelectric power stations. Apart from the existing Qamdo Hydroelectric Power Station, preparations are under way for the construction of the Za Qu River and other big hydroelectric power stations, with a view to building up a power grid centering on the Lancang River in the early 21st century to provide power

Salt pans by the Lancang River in eastern Tibet.

for the forthcoming construction of the Yulong Copper Mine and associated smelting facilities, which are expected to become the economic backbone of Qamdo Prefecture.

Quite a few geothermal spots are located along the "three-river fracture belt," the better-known one being the Quzika Hot Springs in Yanjing ("salt wells") Township by the Lancang River. There are 108 springs there, said to have evolved from teardrops shed by the goddess Dameiyong. The temperature of the spring water ranges between 70 and 25 degrees centigrade. With a moderate temperature and abundant spring water of a low sulfur content, the Quzika Hot Springs appeals to people from far and wide. It is an ideal resort, surrounded by an abundance of walnut, pear, apple and pomegranate trees.

Yanjing Township is a major producer of salt. The many geothermal salt springs here, close to the Lancang River, are the results of fractures caused by neotectonic movements during the Quaternary Period. Some spring water carries salt to the surface as it rises through the Triassic salt-bearing strata. It has a salt content of more than 30 g per liter. Local people have built nearly 2,000 square wooden sheds as salt pans along the river above the spring wells, with their flat tops covered with a 10-cm-thick layer of impermeable red clay. The brine in the pans is left to evaporate in the sun for three to five days until salt crystals are formed. Normally, the February-May period each year is the salt-producing season, when the river water is clear and the salt is white and at its best, while the river water is muddy during the high-water season and the salt is reddish. The annual output of local salt exceeds 300 tons, and it is mostly sold to nearly-by Zayu County, as well as Yunnan's Deqen and Sichuan's Batang counties. Salt was also a major commodity item in the ancient tea-for-horses trade. The brine sheds along the Lancang River are a local tourist attraction.

III. The Lush-Green Bamda Pastures

In the midst of high mountains and deep valleys in the three-river area of Qamdo is a gently sloping, lush-green grassland, which is the famous Bamda Grassland of eastern Tibet. It is located south of Qamdo County and along the upper reaches of the Yu Qu River, a tributary on the eastern flank of the Nujiang River. Under the jurisdiction of Baxoi County and at an altitude exceeding 4,300 m above sea level, it is a flat plateau mountain basin on the main ridge of Mount Taniantaweng, the watershed of the Lancang and Nujiang rivers. The Yu Qu meanders like a jade belt through the central part of the grassland and the broad, low-lying wet land on both banks, overgrown with low and thick meadow plants. Tibetan gazelles can occasionally be spotted in thickets, but they flee in panic the moment a vehicle or tourist draws near. A more common sight is fat Himalayan marmots bustling about near their

The Bamda Grassland.

holes. Of course, rat rabbits are to be seen everywhere.

Although at an high altitude, the Bamda Grassland, lying in eastern Tibet, has a fairly good grass coverage, thanks to slightly greater precipitation than in west-central Tibet, and is one of the better grazing grounds in the autonomous region. Therefore, it has a more developed animal husbandry.

The unique ecological environment enables the Bamda Grassland to be Tibet's main producer of many important and valuable medicinal plants, such as bulb of fritillary, ginseng fruit, rhubarb, large-leafed gentian and rose-boot. The most famous is the Chinese caterpillar fungus, an insect-fungus compound that is very special and valuable in herbal medicine. In winter, it is a silkworm-like insect lying hidden in the shallow soil layer, and in summer, a blade of grass shoots from its head, like a match stick. Therefore, it has the popular name "winter-worm-summer-grass." In fact, it is a combination of the stroma of an ercoth plant and the dead body of its host, batmoth larva. In other words, fungus makes its inroads into the batmoth larva around the time when winter sets in, and after the larva goes underground it gradually dies off as its nutrients are consumed by the fungus. As summer comes, a 10-20 mm fungus stroma grows from the head of the dead body and emerges above the ground like a blade of grass. In appearance, it is half worm and half plant. It is both a medicinal herb and a valuable tonic. It contains fat, course protein, Chinese caterpillar fungus acid, multiple vitamins, animoacids and micronutrients, which are good for regulating the human immune system. As early as in the Ming Dynasty (1368-1644) Chinese caterpillar fungus was already being shipped to Japan. It has gained even greater fame in recent years, and sells well on both domestic and foreign markets.

Chinese caterpillar fungus usually grows in alpine meadows at an altitude of between 3,500 and 5,000 m above sea level. The period from mid-May to early June each year, when the ice and snow melt, is the best time for gathering it. When the time comes, local herdsmen and herbalists, with bamboo baskets on their backs and shovels in their hands, go to the Bamda Grassland, and look for it. When they locate it, they dig 10 to 20 cm deep in order to extract the whole caterpillar fungus. After the soil is carefully removed, it is then wiped clean and dried before it is ready for use as a medicinal herb. Chinese caterpillar fungus becomes a sizeable source of income for the local Tibetan people. Yet, indiscriminate gath-

Chinese caterpillar fungus.

ering damages the grass cover, and has an adverse effect on the fragile ecological environment of the Tibetan plateau.

Snow lotus is a perennial herbaceous plant of the *Saussurea genus*, the composite family growing near the snow line 4,500 m or more above sea level. Ice and snow keep this hardy plant company virtually all the year round, and the latter uses the short period of two to three summer months to sprout, grow up, flower and bear fruit. Its stem is about 10 cm long, and its flower is like a lotus, with rows upon rows of snow-white petals around the receptacles, hence its name. It is also called a "jade rabbit" for its stem is thickly covered with long, white hair, so that it looks like a white rabbit amid the snow-covered mountain folds and gravel. According to the tenets of traditional Tibetan medicine, the snow lotus is good for treating colds and easing expectoration, stimulating male virility, warming up a woman's uterus and treating gynecological diseases. Snow lotus is also prepared in the form of medicinal liquor or injections.

Azaleas and tower-shaped rhubarb in an alpine meadow about 4,200 meters above sea level.

Rose-boot has a special effect on oxygen deficiency and improving the cardiac and neurological vascular functions. It has been widely used in the prevention and treatment of heart diseases in recent years. Oral liquids containing rose-boot extract have proved effective in helping newcomers to the plateau overcome altitude sickness.

The Bamda Grassland is sparsely populated, and only the Sichuan-Tibet and Yunnan-Tibet highways pass through the area. Travelers, whether on horseback or by car, are advised to take oral rose-boot liquid before they set out or carry it with them as a standby medicine against altitude sickness. On their way they may meet herdsmen from time to time, who emerge from their tents to peddle freshly picked caterpillar fungus and snow lotus. They may even offer home-brewed *qingke* wine or a cup of butter-tea.

The Bamda Airport, at an altitude of 4,330 m above sea level, went into service in 1995, linking the town of Qamdo with Chengdu, capital of Sichuan Province. More than 100 km from Qamdo and with a runway 5,500 m in length, it is the highest airport and has the longest runway in the world. The air link has greatly shortened the travel time between Qamdo and Chengdu. A road trip over the 1,200-km distance between the two cities takes at least three days, involving the crossing of five or six high, snow-capped mountains, such as Mts Dagmala, Chola, Zheduo and Qionglai, and big rivers such as the Lancang, Jinsha and Yalong. The flight between the two places takes less than two hours.

IV. The Ancient "Tea-for-Horses" Trade Route

For many years little was known about an ancient trail in the lofty forest-covered mountains in the area where Tibet, Yunnan and Sichuan meet. This is the ancient "tea-for-horses" trade route that meandered through the heartland of the Hengduan Mountains and the thick forests of the Himalayas. For centuries, caravans moving along this route crossed the Yunnan-Guizhou Plateau and the Qinghai-Tibet Plateau, and the Jinsha, Lancang, Nujiang, Yarlung

Zangbo, Yalong and Dadu rivers. It was a trading route traversing the hinterland of East Asia and, like the "Silk Road" in Northwest China, was another major line of communication promoting economic and cultural links among the Han Chinese, Tibetan and other ethnic groups, and playing an important role in promoting the social, economic and cultural development in the Tibetan-inhabited areas in Tibet, Sichuan and Yunnan at that time. It is of major historical and cultural value.

The "tea-for-horses" trading route was in use from the Tang Dynasty (618-907) until the Republican period (1912-1949). Tea produced in Sichuan and Yunnan was carried on horsebacks to Tibet to exchange for Tibetan horses and medicinal herbs. There were in fact two trails: the southern trail (the Yunnan-Tibet trail) and the northern trail (the Sichuan-Tibet trail). The southern trail started from the tea-producing area near Erhai Lake at Dali in western Yunnan, and extended north via Lijiang, Zhongdian, Deqen, Markam and Zhagyab to Qamdo. The northern trail started from the tea-producing area of Ya'an in Sichuan, and extended westward via Kangding, Garze and Dege to Qamdo. After the two trails crossed at Qamdo, they once again branched into two: the northern one leading from Qamdo to Riwoqe, Dengqen, Sog, Lhunzhub and Lhasa, and the southern one leading from Qamdo to Lhorong, Banbar, Lhari, Gongbo'gyamda, Maizhokunggar and Lhasa. However, Lhasa was not the final destination. Some caravans would continue via Gyangze, Yadong and other places in southern Tibet to Bhutan, Sikkim, Nepal and India, and even as far as the Kashmir region.

The history of the "tea-for-horses" trade route may date back to days of exchanges between the Tang court and Tubo (an ancient Tibetan kingdom), when tea was first introduced to Tibet. According to historical records, tea was introduced to Tibet by Princess Wencheng. It then became an indispensable daily drink of the Tibetans and other ethnic minorities in the area, to the extent that they could "not do without it in the morning and evening." This was because the inhabitants of Tibet live in highlands 3,000-4,500 m above sea level, where the air pressure is low, and the climate dry and cold, and people are prone to symptoms resulting from oxygen deficiency and low air pressure. Moreover, traditionally, the Tibetans' main diet was beef, mutton, butter and *qingke*, which are not easily digestible. Tea is rich in biological chemical substances: tannin it contains helps dissolve fat, the theine helps stimulate the nervous system, relieve exhaustion and remove disquiet, and its vitamins help make up the vitamin deficiency resulting from an extreme shortage of vegetables and fruits in the diet of highland inhabitants. Thus, tea began to serve as an economic and cultural bond between the Han Chinese and the Tibetans. Starting in the Tang Dynasty, the central government set up the "Office of Tea and Horses" in Xindian Town, Mingshan County, west of Chengdu, to administer the tea-for-horses trade, which thrived for more than 1,000 years. Mingshan County had a long tea-growing history and its tea, called "southern route border tea," was shipped to Tibet, Qinghai and other border regions, as well as to Nepal and Bhutan. However, the tea-for-horses trade and its special trade route did not attain a large scale until the Song Dynasty. During the Northern Song (960-1127), the government bought more than 20,000 Tibetan horses for tea each year. During the Southern Song Dynasty (1127-1279) the court still bought at least 10,000 horses each year. More than half of the tea produced in Sichuan during the Northern and Southern Song Dynasties, 15,000 tons in total, was sold to Tibet. The tea-for-horses trade reached its zenith during the Ming Dynasty (1368-1644), when the Ming court used tea as an important item for maintaining good relations with the chieftains and the upper strata of the clergy and aristocracy of the Tibetan areas. Therefore, tea was a major bond, not only economic but also political and cultural, between the Han Chinese and the ethnic Tibetans. The tea-for-horses trade thrived also during the Qing Dynasty (1644-1911), thus bringing about an all-round growth of trade between the Hans and the Tibetans.

Even during the Republican Period, when the country was bogged down in inter-warlord strife, which also engulfed Sichuan and Tibet, such non-governmental trade was still active, and continued until the end of the Republican Period. Afterwards, with the rise of modern means of transportation, this ancient trading route which had been in operation for more than 1,000 years and played a major role in promoting exchanges between the Hans and the Tibetans began to lose its importance, and this highest and most arduous ancient trading route in human history fell into oblivion. However, interest in it began to revive in the 1990s. Field surveys by scholars have proved that the various ethnic groups, including the Hans and the Tibetans, were pioneers of this route and that the melting of the cultures of various ethnic groups along the route added a special cultural landscape to the varied natural features of the Qinghai-Tibet Plateau and the Hengduan Mountains.

If one retraces the ancient trading route, one may start from Shangri-la (Zhongdian) in Yunnan, and travel in a northward direction, cross the Baima Snowy Mountains and Mount Moirig on the Yunnan-Tibet border, and reach Yanjing Township, where he or she will be able to have a sip of grape wine at a local Catholic church, in addition to visiting the salt pans. It is said that some French missionaries brought grape seeds and the technique of wine making here in the early 20th century. The grape seeds proved to be adaptable to the local environment, so the local grape wine has something in common with French wine. After leaving Yanjing Township, he or she will reach the top of Mount Hongla (4,200 m above sea level) in the Markam Nature Reserve, and have a commanding view of the undulating peaks and ridges below. With some luck, a rare golden monkey may be glimpsed amid bamboo groves. Further north is the Bamda Grassland, from where a flight back to Chengdu will offer an aerial view of the Hengduan Mountains. The traveler may continue the journey from Bamda to Qamdo, where the northern tea-for-horses trail meets the southern one.

Westward from Bamda, one crosses peaks more than 5,000 m above sea level. The journey then leads down into the Nujiang River valley, which is only something over 2,000 m above sea level, and through Baxoi County to Lake Rawu, which presents a restful and intoxicating scene against a backdrop of snow-capped peaks and tree-covered mountains. Going further west along the Parlung Zangbo from the mouth of the lake, past Bomi and across Mount Seqilha, one arrives at Nyingchi, a lush southern-type area in Tibet. It is a major virgin-forest area. On both banks of the Nyang River is fertile land, with groves of fruit trees.

To the west of Nyingchi lies the holy city of Lhasa.

The northern trail leading into Tibet passes through Ya'an, a city on the Qingyi River, Mount Erlang, which is regarded as the first natural barrier blocking the way to Tibet, Luding and the iron-chain suspension bridge across the Dadu River, both figuring prominently in the Chinese revolution, Kangding, which has gained national fame because of a folk song describing life there, snow-capped Mount Chola, the scenic glacier lake of Xinluhai and Dege County on the Jinsha River, which is famous for its traditional way of printing Tibetan Buddhist scriptures. Although most of the above scenic spots are located within the Garze and Aba (Ngawa) Tibetan autonomous prefectures in Sichuan Province, the northern trail of the ancient tea-for-horses trade route offers a full range of samples of the natural and cultural landscapes of the Hengduan Mountains.

In short, the areas traversed by the ancient tea-for-horses trade route offer varied natural environments and a rich variety of animal and plant resources. They have nurtured the cultures and histories of the Tibetan, Han and many other ethnic groups. The ancient trade route can be said to be a gallery of ethnic national cultures and a golden tourism route in the Tibetan-inhabited areas, promising broad prospects for development. It is an ideal trekking route for explorers.

V. Beautiful Alpine Lakes

Southeast Tibet is noted not only for its high mountains and deep gorges, but also for the many alpine lakes of various sizes that dot the forest-covered mountains. These lakes show a potential for developing into tourist attractions. The better-known lakes are Rawu and Yi'ong.

Rawu Lake lies 350 km southwest of Qamdo, and is an alpine lake in southern Baxoi County at an altitude of 3,850 m. It is accessible by the Sichuan-Tibet Highway. If one starts from the county seat and heads in a southward

Rawu Lake, surrounded by snow-capped mountains and forests.

direction, crossing the 4,400-m-high Mount Anliulha Pass, one will see ahead a vast expanse of water surrounded by towering mountains. This is the famous Rawu Lake. What unfolds ahead is a pastoral scene with distinctive Tibetan highland features: a mirror-like lake surface that reflects the steep, snow-capped peaks surrounding it, pine and cypress woods, grassy lake-side beach land on which cattle and sheep leisurely graze, and plots of farmland under *qingke*, peas and rape.

Rawu Lake is linked with Angong Co upstream and Anqie Co downstream. The three lakes lie like a narrow strip of water in between high mountains, 29 km in total length, less than one km in average width and 22 sq km in area. Rawu is one of the few large lakes in eastern Tibet. It is fed by snowmelt from the surrounding mountains, such as the Boxoila Ridge, the Gabugangri Snowy Mountains and the Arzagonglha Glacier, so the temperature of its water is low, ranging between 6.6 and 15.4 degrees centigrade in summer, while in winter the lake is frozen.

Rawu Lake used to be a river but was blocked by a huge amount of boulders and rocks about 200 years ago when a landslide suddenly occurred at a point near its present outlet, thus forming a river lake as we see it today. It is a typical barrier lake. High waves and rapid water are seen at its outlet, and what flows west is the Parlung Zangbo, the one with the greatest volume of flow among the five major tributaries of the Yarlung Zangbo. So, Rawu Lake is actually the source of the Parlung Zangbo. The lake is not deep, but abounds in scaleless fish, a special product of the highlands.

Leaving Rawu Lake and going down along the Yarlung Zangbo valley past the seat of Bomi County at an altitude of 2,700 m, one gets to another major lake in eastern Tibet — Yi'ong Lake. The 260-km trip includes gorges below steep, snow-capped mountains on both banks of the Parlung Zangbo, that conform to the fracture belt, and the remains of a disastrous landslide at Guxiang in 1952 — boulders and piles of rocks that litter the ground everywhere. This constitutes a somber scene along the Bomi section of the Sichuan-Tibet Highway. On the opposite side of the river is the Gangxiang

Apple trees and wheat intercropped along the Lancang River.

Nature Reserve where one ha of spruce has 3,000 cu m of timber in reserve, four to five times that in the Northeast China forest areas and a rare biological output in the world. Yi'ong Lake along the lower reaches of the Yi'ong Zangbo, a northern tributary of the Parlung Zangbo, lies at 2,200 m above sea level and is an elongated lake running in a northwest-southeast direction. It is another barrier lake resulting from a nearby alpine glacier debris flow blocking the mouth of the Yi'ong Zangbo. The climate here is mild, humid and rainy, because the river and lake have a relatively low elevation and lie close to the corridor for moist air currents along the Great Gorge of the Yarlung Zangbo, so that they are dominated by the warm and moist air currents from the Indian Ocean. Every morning vapor rises from the placid lake surface and hovers over it like a sea of clouds, and the surrounding mountains are shrouded in mist. In contrast to the deep, narrow Parlung Zangbo valley, confined by towering mountain slopes facing each other, the Yi'ong Lake area boasts a large body of water and a high clear sky. Surrounded by tree-covered mountains, it promises to be a tourist attraction and resort, with its charming scenery and pleasant climate.

Thanks to the local mild, humid and misty climate, Yi'ong Lake, although located on the northern side of the Himalayas, still manifests a subtropical scene, like those found south of the mountain range — the mountain slopes surrounding the lake are covered with luxuriant evergreen broadleaf and needle leaf trees, fruits of wild Chinese flowering quince send forth their bracing fragrance, and monkeys frequent the forests. Tea plantations and apple orchards are welcome variations on the lakeside land and woodlands. The green tea produced by the Yi'ong Tea Plantation is of fine quality. The tea bushes are irrigated by snowmelt and basically free from chemical fertilizer and pesticides, so that the tea is virtually free from pollution. It already enjoys a good reputation on the domestic market. Tea plantations are still small in scale, with the total acreage amounting to not much more than ten ha, and output is likewise limited. Its annual production is 100,000 kg. As the only tea-producing area in Tibet, the place has a broad prospects for development.

The Yi'ong tea plantation.

Some lesser-known lakes in eastern Tibet also have the potential for developing into tourist attractions. For example, Marco Lake southeast of the county seat (Gartog) of Markam has an area of 18 sq km and lies at an altitude of 4,300 m above sea level. Although it is high and has few trees, it has a great variety of fish and the two islets in the heart of the lake are habitats for wild ducks and migratory birds, which together with the blue lake water and alpine meadows around form an attractive alpine lake scenery. Also, the lake group in Lhorong County, popularly known as the "21 Taras (varied forms of the Goddess of Mercy)," consists of innumerable small lakes, including Choma Langco, which is the source of the river of the same name, a tributary of the Nujiang River, as well as other small alpine lakes, including the three lakes of Puyu south of the seat of Banbar County, which constitute the source of a Nujiang tributary, the Mai Qu. The three lakes are referred to as the White, Yellow and Black lakes, due to their different depths, varieties of aqueous plants and rock strata of the lake walls. The White Lake has a 20-m-high waterfall cascading into it. These beautiful lakes have not been commercially developed because they are relatively inaccessible.

VI. Zayu County — Southern-Style Scenery

Zayu County is located south of Rawu Lake and separated from it by the 4,700-m-high Demo La Pass. Popularly known as "Tibet's Jiangnan (referring to the areas south of the Yangtze River renowned for their lush scenery)," Zayu, meaning "a place where humans live" in Tibetan, is under the jurisdiction of Nyingchi Prefecture.

Zayu is located on the southeast inclined plane of the Tibetan plateau, where the Himalayas and the Hengduan Mountains meet, with the north at a higher altitude than the south. There are big ups and downs in terrain, showing a great altitudinal difference. There is a height difference of at least 4,000 m from the top of the mountains to the lowest point of the river valleys at an altitude of 1,400 m above sea level. There are more than ten peaks in Zayu exceeding 5,000 m above sea level. The highest is the Moirig Snow Mountain, standing 6,740 m above sea level in the area where eastern Zayu, Zogang County and Yunnan's Deqen County meet. It enjoys wide fame as a holy mountain.

Conforming to the terrain, the Zayu River flows from north to south, and eventually joins the Brahmaputra River in India. Under the influence of the Indian Ocean's warm air currents from the south, Zayu has a mild and humid climate, with an average annual temperature of 10-20 degrees centigrade and

Rice paddies and virgin forests by the Zayu Qu River.

Moirig Snow Mountain.

an average annual rainfall of approximately 1,000 mm. Thanks to the ample hydro-thermal resources, it is an ideal place for growing paddy rice as well as corn, wheat and a variety of subtropical fruits and vegetables. Two rice crops are reaped a year in Zayu. Terraced rice fields extend from the riverside all way up high slopes, resembling the lush scenes south of the Yangtze River.

Zayu is also rich in forest resources, with 120 million cu m in timber reserve. The great height difference gives rise to a remarkable altitudinal differentiation of natural vegetative landscapes. Generally speaking, the mountainous areas below 2,600 m above sea level are home to typical subtropical broadleaf forests, including such valuable varieties as *Phoebe zhennan*, camphor and banana shrub (*Michelia figo*), while the slopes facing the sun are covered with high Yunnan pine forests of single species, together with pockets of bamboo, bajiao banana, palm and other trees of economic value. The mountains above 2,600-3,200 m above sea level are clothed with mixed warm temperate needle leaf-broadleaf mixed forests comprising alpine pine, hemlock, oak and birch. The mountains, ranging between 3,200 and 4,000 m in altitude, are home to sub-alpine cold temperate dark conifers, notably spruce and fir forests. Higher up than this come an azalea shrub meadows belt, sparse cushion-shape plants belt and permafrost belt, in that order.

Living in these thick forests and grassy areas are animals on the national protection list, such as Bengal tiger, goral, brown bear, macaque, lesser panda, *Moschus berezovskii*, flying squirrel, red-billed leiothrix, blue-throated sunbird and red-bellied parrot.

Nature reserves with a total area of 1,014 sq km were established in Cibagou, Shizhu Village and Lhamunongbagou in Zayu in 1985 in an effort to protect the special natural environment, ecosystem, and valuable and rare animals there. The Cibagou Nature Reserve, the largest of the three and with an area of 1,002 sq km, has a complete range of subtropical forest ecosystem types, together with special plant and rare animal species. The Shizhu Village Nature Reserve, only 5.4 sq km in area, preserves primitive Yunnan pine forests of single species. The forest facies is tidy, and most trees are more than 60 m tall and 170 cm in diameter. The total standing timber in the reserve is 200,000 cu m, averaging more than 1,200 cu m per ha, far surpassing the resources of Korean pines in the northeast China forest areas. It is a high-yield Yunnan pine forest rarely seen elsewhere in the world. The Lhamunongbagou Nature Reserve is 6.6 sq km in area. Among the typical evergreen broadleaf trees growing there are Yunnan *nanmu*, toon, laurel family, *Ping machilus* and fragrant cinnamon, as well as apple fig, *manyprickle acanthopanax*, kiwi and other major fruit trees and resources of medicinal herbs.

Zayu County is also where people of the Deng ethnic minority live in compact communities. The Deng used to live in dense forests, leading a primitive slash-and-burn life, by gathering fruit and hunting animals. They have always had their own language, which is of the Tibeto-Burmese subfamily of the Chinese-Tibetan family of languages, they did not have a script in the old days, and so they used to keep records by tying knots or cutting marks on poles. After the founding of the People's Republic of China, the People's Government helped them to leave the forests and settle in hamlets built by the government, thus ending their primitive life style. With help from the government, they learned to tend crop fields and tea plantations, so that they are now able to lead a secure life. Since China began its reform and opening-up program, the Dengs have adopted new farming techniques and developed a diversified economy, resulting in remarkably higher incomes and living standards. Many families have bought television sets and VCD players, 90 percent and more of school-age children are enrolled in schools, and several dozen out of a population of 1,300 people are now government employees. Visitors to a Deng people's hamlet will see wooden houses, gardens with flowers and other plants, and pens filled with pigs and poultry. The blue sky, white clouds, snow-topped peaks, lush forests and golden rice crops in the terraced paddy fields — all these make a peaceful picture. Local people say that the word Deng has the meaning of a poor person in their language, but now, they explain, it should take on a meaning of a happy person.

Deng women usually wear silver earrings in the shape of a bugle, and a necklace of pearls or silver ornaments. Deng men wear a black turban and carry a long knife at the waist.

VII. Wonders of Maritime Glaciers

Nyingchi and Qamdo prefectures in eastern Tibet not only have expansive primitive forests, they also boost extensive monsoon maritime glaciers, due to the fact that under the influence of the south-westerly monsoon winds from the Indian Ocean and, to some extent, the south-easterly monsoon winds from the Pacific Ocean, the climate in these two prefectures is mild and humid, and there is considerable rainfall. The tops of many peaks are perpetually covered in snow, and valley glaciers are large in area and varied in type. For example, there are maritime valley glaciers in the southeastern section of the Nyainqentanglha Mountains, the eastern section of the Himalayas and the Hengduan Mountains. These glaciers exist by relying mainly on replenishment by ample rainfall and snowfall, because these mountains receive a large amount of snowfall and the snowline is lower than in other places, ranging between 4,500 m and 5,000 m above sea level. They are characterized by a fairly high temperature on the ice surface and a fairly strong glacial dissipation, so that they advance or retreat by leaps and bounds, generally showing a fast pace of downward movement, at an average annual pace of 100-300 m. For example, the Kaqin Glacier, located in the southern flank of the

Nyainqentanglha Mountains, is 35 km long and covers an area of 172 sq km, larger than the largest glacier in the Alps, the Aletsch Glacier. The lower end of the Kaqin Glacier's tongue drops to an altitude of 2,530 m, extending well into the primitive forests. Uniquely, the glacier winds through green forests like a giant white snake.

There are 898 glaciers, including the Kaqin, on the south flank of the eastern section of the Nyainqentanglha Mountains, with an aggregate area of 2,394 sq km, approximately accounting for 41 per cent of the total area of glaciers in the mountain range. This area is one of the strongest glaciation centers among the medium-low latitude areas in the northern hemisphere. This shows the strong influence of the warm, wet monsoon air currents from outside on glacial development in this area.

Glaciers serve as "solid-state reservoirs," and are a very valuable water resource on the plateau. They are the main source of replenishments for all the rivers and lakes on the plateau.

So eastern Tibet is an area with a concentration of six glacier zones — the glaciers zone along the Yi'ong Zangbo valley; the Bode Zangbo glaciers zone, the Yupu Zangbo glaciers zone; the Rawu Lake valley glaciers zone; the Mount Namjagbarwa glaciers zone; and the Mount Jialabailei glaciers zone. Together, they constitute a well-known monsoon maritime glaciers community and the largest-scale glaciers community of this type in China.

There are 45 glaciers in the Rawu Lake zone along the upper reaches of the Parlung Zangbo, with a total area of 418 sq km. One valley glacier, the Yalong (also known as the Laigu) glacier, has its upper limit at 6,508 m above sea level. It consists of six branch glaciers, with gray-black median moraines between them. It is quite a spectacle to see white glaciers and black median moraines snaking down the mountains side by side. Its end tip is at an altitude of 3,960 m, with its two flanks covered with forests and farmland. It is a world of white above and the Rawu Lake below. The Yalong Glacier is 36 km long, and covers an area of 175.3 sq km, ranking as the largest valley glacier in eastern Tibet and indeed on the whole Tibet plateau in terms of both length and size. The melted water from ice and snow all flows into Rawu Lake. There is another glacier nearby in the same valley, the well-known Arza Glacier, which is about 20 km long. Its end tip is at an altitude of 2,400 m, so that the lower section of the glacier is already within the needle leaf-broadleaf mixed forests. It is the lowest-altitude glacier in Tibet. Owing to the fact that the temperature of the ice surface is not very low, ice earthworms and ice fleas are commonly found there. The Arza Glacier is located near 29° N, but its end tip is even lower in altitude than those of the glaciers of Mount Bogda in the Tianshan Mountains in Xinjiang, lying close to 44° N. This is a special phenomenon among China's modern glaciers.

Namjagbarwa seen from a *mani* stone mound.

Mount Namjagbarwa, situated by the Great Canyon on the lower reaches of the Yarlung Zangbo, is the highest peak at the eastern end of the Himalayas. With an elevation of 7,782 m above sea level, it has 41 glaciers around its main peak, with a total area of 222.21 sq km. One of the glaciers has a drop of 4,882 m from its source to its end tip, some 1,200 m more than the vertical height difference (3,648 m) of the well-known Rongpu Glacier on the northern slope of Mount Qomolangma, which is indeed a world record. What is more astonishing is the fact that on the western slope of the main peak is a glacier capable of saltation. Called the Zelongnong Glacier, it is 10.25 km long and covers an area of 17.9 sq km. What makes it different from other glaciers is the fact that its advance or retreat is not entirely controlled by the changes in the hydrothermal conditions, and that when it moves downwards it leaps in an unusual way, with a speed and manner rarely seen elsewhere in the country. Its abrupt leaping downward movement often causes destruction of houses and farmland, as well as human casualties, without warning.

There are nine valley glaciers in the glaciers zone of Mount Jialabailei, opposite Mount Namjagbarwa. Their combined area is 149 sq km. The Zhong'aijiedo Glacier, on the eastern slope, is 14.7 km long and covers an area of 31.25 sq km. With its end tip at an altitude of 2,600 m, it is one of the few large valley glaciers in China with an extremely low end tip.

The Yupu Zangbo glaciers zone covers 400 sq km in area, with at least eight valley glaciers each exceeding five km in length. The Midui Glacier, on the southern bank of the Yupu Zangbo, is a 10.2-km-long compound glacier, with its two branch glaciers meeting in the form of two 700-m-high ice cascades at a point of 4,100 m above sea level, to become a single tongue. Between the two ice cascades is a small ridge inselberg of basal complex, the middle and lower parts of which are covered with virgin forests. The stubborn green life on this islet surrounded by a world of ice is amazing, and is possible only in this type of maritime glacier zone. In addition, below the ice cascades, a beautiful and magnificent glacial arcuate-arched structure can be seen, which is the most beautiful and rare glacial arcuate-arched structure in China. This special structure is the result of the fast melting and rapid downward movement of the Midui Glacier. When it moves downwards, the flanks of the glacier move more slowly than the central part, and likewise the end tip moves more slowly than the upper section. This results in the formation of an arch protrusion on the surface of the middle section. Moreover, for the same reason, the Midui Glacier also moves by leaps, like the Zelongnong Glacier.

Among the 898 glaciers in the Yi'ong Zangbo glaciers zone is the 14-km-long Roguo Glacier, which is flanked by bamboo groves, forests and pastures. The valley echoes with the deafening booming of avalanches, trickling of water, whistling of the wind in the bamboo groves, mooing of cattle, bleating of sheep and human laughter.

The monsoon maritime glaciers in eastern Tibet are a focus of attention in the earth sciences community for their large area, strong activity and many special features. The spectacles of many ice tongues extending into virgin forests are special tourist attractions.

VIII. The Shangri-la in Tibet

Since English writer James Hilton mentioned what he referred to as Shangri-la in the depths of the Himalayas in his novel *Lost Horizon* in 1933, a world-wide search has been touched off for this imaginary paradise on earth. Shangri-la is a fictional place the description of which was probably based on rel-

Springtime in Shangri-la.

evant records and travelogues of scholars and travelers who had been to Tibet. Although Hilton never had. However, many places in the Himalayas answer to his description of Shangri-la, with its snow-capped peaks, expansive grasslands, fertile farmland, imposing and dangerous gorges, and beautiful lakes and forests. In fact, some countries close to the Himalayas have announced that Shangri-la was based on a certain place in the Himalayan area within their territories. For example, in 1992, Nepal's tourism authority announced that a small town on its northern border was the prototype of Shangri-la. But the geographical features and cultural landscapes of these so-called Shangri-la's are grossly at odds with the descriptions in the novel. During the 1980s and 1990s, many Chinese stated that a true Shangri-la should be somewhere in the Tibetan-inhabited areas in China's western region, including the Himalayan area of Tibet and adjacent areas, such as Lijiang or Zhongdian in Deqen Prefecture, Bingzhongluo in Nujiang Prefecture in northwest Yunnan Province, or Daocheng or some other place in southwest Sichuan Province. These places all have snow-capped mountains, lakes, big gorges, forests, pastures, fertile land, and old temples and other venerable buildings, and their cultural and geographical features are closer to Hilton's description. Zhongdian and its vicinity, in particular, boast the great gorges of the Jinsha and Lancang rivers, the pyramid-like Moirig Snowy Mountain, the lush Zhongdian pastures, forest-girt Bitahai Lake, the magnificent Gadam Songtsen Gling Temple ("Guihua Temple" in Chinese, and known as the Lesser Potala to the local people), simple Catholic churches and the ancient town of Zhongdian. The Tibetan, Naxi, Bai and other ethnic groups with different cultures and religious beliefs live in harmony here. All this constitutes a peaceful, quiet utopia. The cultural and geographical landscapes here are almost entirely in accord with the description of Shangri-la in the novel. In 1997, the government of Yunnan Province announced to the world that Shangri-la was in Deqen, and not long afterwards Deqen Prefecture's Zhongdian County was officially renamed Shangri-la County.

Actually, Shangri-la, this beautiful and lovely place, is fictional after all, and the cultural and geographical landscapes of Zhongdian and its vicinity are no more than close to the descriptions of it. If one is to look for a place that matches the descriptions strictly, one must go to the Himalaya Mountains in Tibet, for Deqen does not lie within the scope of the Himalayas. Moreover, many places in Tibet may be found to resemble the descriptions at least in terms of natural geographical landscape, especially in the densely forested high mountains of southeast Tibet, for example, Nyingchi and Mainling along the lower Nyang River and Bomi on the middle reaches of Parlung Zangbo. In such areas, one may see towering snow-capped peaks like Mount Namjagbarwa and Mount Jialabailei, the rapids and gorges of the Parlung Zangbo, and the world's deepest gorge, the Great Canyon of the Yarlung Zangbo, as well as extensive virgin forests and rare ancient cypresses more than 1,000 years old. As for picturesque alpine lakes, such as Basum Co, Yi'ong and Rawu, some visitors have compared them to those of Switzerland. In addition, expansive pastures and farmland on both banks of the Nyang River, groves of apple, pear, peach and walnut trees that dot the fields, roadsides and courtyards of houses are all reminiscent of southern-style scenery. At harvest time, the local people can be seen gathering in wheat or rape while singing. People here live and work in peace and contentment, holding themselves aloof from the world. How similar it is to Shangri-la! In fact, before the Sichuan-Tibet Highway that goes through Nyingchi and Bomi was built, the area was virtually cut off from the outside world, accessible only by the ancient "tea-for-horses" trade route and visited only by some caravans making their way through high mountains and deep gorges.

It should be noted that only a few years ago local residents discovered in the Himalayas south of the Mainling County seat and in the Nyainqentanglha Mountains north of the Bomi County seat the wreckage of airplanes belonging to the U.S. air force which flew war supplies to China over the Himalayas during the Second World War. These airplanes crashed when carrying out missions over the so-called "Hump." This fits in with the forced landing of the airplane carrying the novel's hero at Shangri-la in the opening chapter, and is evidence that the Nyingchi-Mainling-Bomi area was the prototype of Shangri-la in Hilton's novel.

Seven

PROTECTING THE LAST UN-SPOILED HIGHLAND

As the roof of the world, the Tibetan plateau is the earth's highest region, and its natural environment has special features of its own, such as being subnival and having a fairly dry climate; thin air with a low oxygen content; strong solar radiation; clear horizontal and vertical spatial variations; special and varied natural ecosystems; few human activities; and a relatively well-preserved highland natural ecological environment. However, the formation of the Tibetan plateau has a short history, and its natural ecological environment is quite fragile. When subject to outside interference by, for instance, human activity, it is vulnerable to all kinds of changes to varying extents, or even serious, irreversible worsening. Especially with the advent of global warming during the 20th century, the short-term climate on the Tibetan plateau has shown a tendency to become warmer and drier. This will have a negative impact on the ecological environment. In such circumstances, the Tibetan plateau as one of the few unspoiled lands on earth requires extra protection from us in the way of minimizing environmentally unfriendly practices.

I. The Call of the People

Tibet is the habitat of many rare wild animals. There are many examples of animals being captured or killed for their meat, hides, plumage or medicinal usage. The most striking example is the situation of the Tibetan antelope.

The Tibetan antelope is under threat from poachers.

As early as in 1979, the Tibetan antelope was put on the banned list of wildlife trade under the Convention on International Trade in Endangered Species of Wild Fauna and Flora. But starting from the mid-1980s products of its wool (mainly Shahtoosh) began to sell well on the international market. In 1996, a Shahtoosh shawl sold for as much as 3,500 pounds sterling on the London market. Its price has risen to 40,000 U.S. dollars on the European market today. This has led to higher prices for the raw wool illegally exported from Tibet to India for processing. High profits have driven businessmen who are bent solely on making profits to engage in trade in Tibetan antelope wool in total disregard of the international convention. The illegal trade in Shahtoosh is still rampant worldwide.

These merchants have even concocted stories to justify their illegal acts, claiming that Tibetan antelopes often rub their hair against shrubs and rocks during the biannual hair-shedding seasons and that the wool so shed is blown by the wind into balls and collected by herdsmen from the grassland. In fact, the Tibetan antelope wool, referred to as "soft gold" and "fiber diamonds," has been removed from the carcasses of poached Tibetan antelopes. Normally

Slain Tibetan antelopes.

only 125-150 grams of wool can be gathered from one Tibetan antelope, and one Shahtoosh shawl takes the lives of three to five Tibetan antelopes. Because wool taken in winter is of the best quality, the poachers engage in wanton hunting and killing during winter and the lambing season. At night, they stealthily enter areas with a concentration of Tibetan antelopes, turn on the headlights of their vehicles, and, when the startled antelopes flee in panic, they follow in hot pursuit and open fire frenziedly. They skin the dead antelopes and remove the hair from them on the spot. Many young antelopes, deprived of the care of their mothers, are left to starve to death.

During the 1980s, herds of 1,000 to 2,000 Tibetan antelopes each were spotted. But in recent years, a herd of 100 has been a rare sight, as a result of reckless poaching. The number of these animals has dropped from an estimated several million in the early 20th century to just over 100,000 now. According to an estimate based on the amount of Tibetan antelope wool processed in India, at least 20,000 Tibetan antelopes are killed every year. If poaching is allowed to continue at this pace, they will be extinct within 20 years.

China is a signatory to the Convention on International Trade in Endangered Species of Wild Fauna and Flora, and has made tremendous efforts to clamp down on the poaching of Tibetan antelopes. Since 1992, the relevant government departments in Qinghai Province and the Xinjiang and Tibet autonomous regions in China have launched an anti-poaching drive, in which dozens of cases of illegally poaching Tibetan antelopes and trafficking in and smuggling their wool and hides have been uncovered. In October 1999, an international symposium was held in Xining, capital of Qinghai, to discuss the protection of Tibetan antelopes and control of the trade in their hair. The Xining Declaration on the subject emerged from the symposium, stating that the consumer market of Tibetan antelope wool and its derivatives, especially Shahtoosh shawls, and the high profits resulting from them are the fundamental cause of the continuous, large-scale poaching of wild Tibetan antelopes, and that the abolition of all processing of Tibetan antelope wool and trade in its finished goods needs greater political commitment and cooperation in political will, finance and techniques on the part of the processing countries and consumer countries. The declaration explicitly defined the responsibilities of the countries of distribution, transit countries and trading and consumer countries in the protection of Tibetan antelopes and the control of the trade in their wool, calling on the relevant countries to provide a strict legal framework in this regard.

Since 1993, Tibet and Qinghai have set up the Changtang and Hoh Xil nature reserves, with a combined area of 383,000 sq km with the emphasis on protecting the Tibetan antelope and the ecosystem of the grassland, its habitat.

Despite these efforts, the poaching of Tibetan antelopes and the processing of and trade in Tibetan antelope wool products are still rampant. As an official with the implementing body of the Convention put it, he and his colleagues have reason to believe that France is continuing with this trade, and so are Britain and other European countries.

II. Quiet Changes in the Environment

The fact that the formation of its present-day geographical environment of the Tibetan plateau has a short history means that the local ecosystem is fragile and unstable. With global warming, the temperature on the plateau has been on a slow rise over the past few decades. This is bound to bring about corresponding changes in the natural geographical process, such as the shrinking of the tundra on the plateau; the shrinking and retreating of lakes or evolution into salt lakes; accelerated dissipation of glaciers; and the weakening of bogginess, with the result that desertification and other changes in the natural ecological environment will be aggravated.

Furthermore, such changes have been worsened by reckless human behavior, resulting in desertification, and water and soil erosion.

The Qinghai-Tibet Plateau is among the areas with fairly serious desertification in China. Although it is Qinghai Province that is mostly affected, desertification in some parts of Tibet should nevertheless not be overlooked. For example, the land affected by desertification in the valleys of the Yarlung Zangbo on its upper and middle reaches and its tributaries amounts to 3.14 million ha, more than half of which is shifting sand dunes and exposed gravel ground. Sand along the riverbanks has even spread to the waists of riverside mountain slopes. A number of towns, like the seat of Zhongba County on the upper reaches of Yarlung Zangbo, have been deserted in face of the irresistible advance of sand dunes. Desertification has resulted in the damage of fertile farmland, degeneration of natural pastures and destruction of houses and roads. It is not only a serious threat to the production and life of the people in the affected areas, but also a notable indicator of the degenerated environment in these places.

Apart from the warming and drying of the plateau in recent decades as a natural factor, the human destructive factor, such as overgrazing of natural pastures and over-gathering of firewood and grass, is also a very important cause of the worsening desertification. For example, large tracts of natural pastures in Nagqu in northern Tibet have become inferior as a result of overgrazing, to the extent of desertification in some cases. The degeneration of pastures is a prelude to desertification and timely measures must be taken to stop overgrazing and promote rotation grazing and the close-off of pastures to facilitate recovery of the pastures, so as to hold desertification in check.

Although Tibet has some reserves of coal, petroleum and natural gas, it is far from meeting the fuel needs of the local peasants and herdsmen because of the limited reserves and low level of exploitation. For example, 96 percent of the cooking fuel consumption in the rural areas around Lhasa, Xigaze and Shannan on the middle reaches of the Yarlung Zangbo is bio-energy, such as firewood, crop stalks, dried cow dung and grass roots; firewood makes up one-third of the 55,000 tons of fuel consumed every year, which means that about 4,000-7,000 ha of shrubs are destroyed every year, inevitably resulting in further desertification.

China is one of the world's countries with serious water and soil erosion. Although Tibet is not among the worst-affected areas in China, serious ero-

Soil erosion in a deforested region between the Salween (Nu or Chiama Ngu Chu) and Mekong (Lancang or Zaqu) rivers in 1996.

sion does occur on a local scale as a result of the excessive cutting of trees, deforestation for land reclamation and gathering of large quantities of firewood, which has destroyed vegetation. A case in point is the valleys of the "three rivers" area in southeastern Tibet that comprises the western part of the Hengduan Mountains. Not only does the ecology of these valleys tend toward desertification, but also landfalls and mudslides occur frequently on slopes along many sections of the rivers. Another example is the "area of one river plus two tributaries" on the middle reaches of the Yarlung Zangbo. Every year, the amount of silt flowing into the Yarlung Zangbo exceeds 50 million tons because the cover of natural forests in this area was thin in the first place, and the vegetation cover has been further reduced by excessive gathering of firewood.

The degeneration of pastures and reduction of forests on the plateau have had a significant impact on the ecological environment of the wild fauna and flora, making the conditions of their habitats inferior and the scope of their existence increasingly smaller. This, plus the serious poaching of wild animals and excessive gathering of wild plants over the past few decades, has grossly damaged the resources of wild animals and plants on the plateau, resulting not only in a sharp reduction in numbers but also leaving some individual species on the brink of extinction. In addition to the poaching of Tibetan antelopes, many similar cases of deprivation have occurred on the plateau. For example, musk deer, Chinese caterpillar fungus, the bulb of fritillary and other valuable medicinal herbs, and hides of Himalayan marmots and muntjacs had always been local specialties but are now in short supply as a result of excessive gathering and poaching, so that their prices have shot up. As for the Changtang plateau in the heartland of the plateau, which had long been known as a "natural game park," human economic activities, such as salt production, seasonal grazing, hunting and transportation, has forced most of the wild animals, including wild Tibetan yaks, asses and antelopes to retreat to the "no-man's land" north of the Nagqu-Ngari Highway, that is, approximately north of 33° N.

In addition to the above obvious changes, pollution from waste water, waste gas and waste materials is increasing notably in some areas on this "unspoiled plateau" which had known little pollution before. This is because of the exploitation of mineral and other resources, swift expansion of industrial and agricultural production, and growth of the urban population over the past few decades. Of course, environmental pollution on a local scale has not gone to the extent of bringing marked changes to the natural environment of the Tibetan plateau as a whole. The plateau is still a piece of unspoiled land, keeping its ecological environment basically intact.

III. Arduous Course for Achieving Harmony Between Man and Nature

The relationship among population, resources, environment and development is a topic that various countries all over the world are concerned with. Environment and resources are the necessary conditions for human existence and development. To an area like Tibet, with a special but fragile ecological environment, it is all the more necessary to harmonize the relations among resources, environment and social development. Therefore, it is a very important and arduous task to preserve the ecological environment of the Tibetan plateau in the course of exploiting its natural resources and developing it's the economy, and construct a good relationship by which human beings and Nature can coexist in harmony.

Tibet will focus on the following aspects in view of the current conditions with regard to the environment of the plateau:

(1) Improving the conditions in the nature reserves

The purpose of establishing a nature reserve is to protect the primitive "background" of the numerous vastly diverse natural ecosystems and their special natural worlds as well as the existing resources of rare and endangered wild fauna and flora on the plateau. It serves as a research base and a natural laboratory for the study of alpine biology and earth sciences, and as a testing ground in the quest for a relationship of harmonious development among the utilization and protection of natural resources, human economic activities and the natural environment. It also serves as a natural classroom and museum of popular science concerning nature, the environment and resources, in the interest of raising the local people's awareness the importance of environmental protection and their general knowledge. Some nature reserves are also suitable for ecological tours and exploration.

So far, Tibet has established 18 nature reserves, with a combined area of 400,800 sq km, accounting for 33.4 percent of the autonomous region's territory. This percentage is higher than that of any other province or autonomous regions in the country. Four of them are at the national level: the Mount Qomolangma Nature Reserve, with the highest altitude in the world; the Changtang Nature Reserve and the Markam Yunnan Golden Monkeys Nature Reserve, the world's largest game parks of alpine rare animals; and the Medog Nature Reserve, where the world's No. 1 Great Canyon is located. They are internationally known. Undoubtedly, they can serve as models for the effective protection of the diversity of the fauna and flora on the plateau, and ensure the sustainable utilization of bio-resources and a benign cycle of the natural ecology.

While setting up nature reserves and clamping down on the poachers of key nationally protected wild animals, the state will also allocate a large sum of money for setting up a "Tibetan Antelope Artificial Breeding and Research Center" and a base for returning artificially bred Tibetan antelopes to the wild. To be located in Damxung County under Lhasa City and in Gaco Township in the Shuanghu Special Administrative District under Nagqu Prefecture, the center and base are aimed at protecting this endangered species and implementing a program for the rational utilization and commercial production of Tibetan antelope wool resources.

(2) Protecting natural forests and afforesting barren mountains

In view of the serious water and soil erosion in the Hengduan Mountains in eastern Tibet and the deteriorating ecological environment of the mountainous areas, especially valleys, the three counties in Qamdo Prefecture located on the upper reaches of the Yangtze River — Markam, Jomda and Gonjo — in 1999 ceased commercial felling of natural forests, closed 18 timber mills and three timber exchanges in the area, in an effort to protect the natural forests on the upper reaches of the Yangtze. At the same time, great efforts have been made to plant trees on barren mountains so as to expand the vegetation cover for better water and soil conservation. Of course, as part of the protective and ecological forest belt project on the upper reaches of the Yangtze, which is among the national key projects for ecological improvement, the protection of the natural forests in the eastern Tibet's mountainous areas should also include land improvement (such as terracing of land on slopes, building dykes to protect riverside land and constructing ponds and reservoirs), planting fast-growing trees for firewood, opening of orchards and diversification of the economy, so as to meet the rural residents' need for cooking fuel

A protective forest belt is taking shape along the Yarlung Zangbo.

and increase their incomes while holding the deterioration of the mountainous area environment in check.

(3) Rationally utilizing natural pastures and accelerating construction of artificial pastures

Tibet has vast expanses of natural pastures, but they have seriously degenerated and been badly affected by desertification. In order to effectively hold desertification in check and utilize pastoral resources in a sustainable manner, it is essential to construct artificial winter and spring pastures, in addition to controlling the cattle population appropriately, developing natural pasture resources rationally and restoring the productivity of the pastures by raising cattle and sheep in sheds and pens, and sealing off pastures to protect them. The aim of these measures is to increase fodder production to meet the demand in winter and spring, and reduce the pressure on the supporting capacity of the natural pastures, so as to slow down their degeneration and desertification, and effectively improve the ecological environment of the grassland.

(4) Stepping up construction of farmland protective forest belts

In areas seriously affected by wind and sand storms along the middle reaches of the Yarlung Zangbo, a multi-purpose system of protective forest belts is needed to improve and protect the ecological environment of the river valleys, in order to hold desertification in check and reduce the harm caused by wind and sand storms to farmland, houses and roads. This system should focus on the protection of farmland while also increasing the resources of firewood, timber, fruit trees and trees for special purposes, combining forests, shrubs and grass. The plan formulated in the 1990s for comprehensive development and environmental control of the area of "one river plus two tributaries" set the goals to be achieved by the year 2000: the building of fodder-production bases with an area of 480 ha and enclosing more than 20,000 ha of pastures affected by desertification for protection, so as to raise the tree coverage rate in this area from 2.4 percent to 3.21 percent; and in areas of busy productive activities, the coverage rate of planted trees should rise from the original 1.78 percent to 9.64 percent, so as to achieve marked economic and social as well as ecological benefits. So far, most items on the plan have been put into implementation, and have yielded fairly good results. For example, the artificial protective tree belt from Xigaze to Zetang, several hundred km long, is playing a positive role in effectively regulating the climatic environment of the valleys, as indicated by the conspicuous drop in the average speed of wind and remarkably fewer sandy days. At present, Lhasa has 32 fewer sandy days than it had 30 years ago; Xigaze, 34 days; and Zetang, 32 days. Rainfall is also notably higher than the average a few years ago, and the humidity level has risen. In 2002, the number of days with excellent-good air quality and minimal-light air pollution in Lhasa had increased noticeably, with the rate of excellent-good days amounting to 98 percent. Meanwhile, a new plan for environmental improvement is being formulated.

Other measures include intensified sewage treatment and comprehensive utilization of garbage in Lhasa, Xigaze, Qamdo and other major towns, strict control of paper-making, chemical and other polluting industrial projects, improvement of the environment of mining areas, and development of hydropower, geothermal and solar energy to reduce the consumption of biofuels like trees, shrubs and grass.

Despite enhanced awareness of the importance of protecting the natural resources and ecological environment of the plateau on the part of the local government and people, the many efforts they have made in this respect and the many gratifying achievements they have made so far, the people of the plateau still feel unequal, in terms of manpower, to the changes that are taking place quietly to the ecological environment of the plateau, which is so vast and sparsely populated. Take the valley of the Yarlung Zangbo for example. Although much has been done to combating desertification, the area still faces a grim situation because it is still hard to fundamentally hold in check the natural factors behind desertification (such as the negative impact of global warming on the environmentally vulnerable "roof of the world"). Therefore, it requires not only a large amount of funds, but also an enormous amount of labor and effort to build a harmonious relationship between man and nature on the plateau.

Appendix

VARIETIES AND DISTRIBUTION OF NATURAL RESOURCES IN TIBET

1. Pastures

The pastures of various types in Tibet cover a total area of 65 million ha, of which 99.4 percent are natural pastures. Utilizable pastures amount to 60.36 million ha, accounting for 27.1 percent of the national total in the same category.

The largest share is subnival pastures, which account for about 38.9 percent of the total in Tibet. They are distributed mainly in the semi-arid areas in the central and western parts of the plateau, including the greater part of Nagqu Prefecture and Xigaze, Shannan and Ngari prefectures. The grass here is mainly needle grass, only about 20-40 cm high, with a coverage rate of 30-50 percent and a yield of 700-1,300 kg of fresh grass per ha. It contains 10-16 percent of coarse protein and 30 percent of coarse fiber, and is of fair quality, suitable for grazing Tibetan sheep.

Next come subnival meadows, which account for 31.3 percent of the total pastureland in Tibet and are mainly distributed in the semi-warm, semi-humid areas in the eastern part of Nagqu Prefecture and Nyingchi and Qamdo prefectures. This type of meadow is of a variety of sagebrush and herbaceous plants of the sedge family. Since the grass grows close to the ground, its coverage rate is as high as 80-90 percent. It contains as much as 16 percent or more of coarse protein, while its content of coarse fiber can drop to below 15 percent. So it is soft, tasty and fairly suitable for grazing yaks and Tibetan sheep. This type of grass has a higher output, with one ha of pasture yielding 1,500-2,200 kg of fresh grass annually.

There are other types of alpine pastures, such as mountain shrubby grass, subnival desert and subnival desert-steppe. Among the better pastures are also marshy meadows distributed in low wetlands along rivers and lakes, which yield more than 2,500 kg of fresh sagebrush and other varieties of grass per ha annually. They are good winter and spring grazing grounds, and sometimes their grass is cut for fodder. However, they are limited in acreage.

2. Forests

Thick natural forests are distributed in the Tibetan portion of the Hengduan Mountains in the eastern part of the plateau as well as the Himalaya Mountains on its southern edge. They are the only well-preserved large tracts of virgin forests still existing in China, an important part of the southwest China forest area and second only to the northeast China forest area. There are 12.67 million ha of forests throughout Tibet, accounting for about 10 percent of Tibet's total land area. Timber in reserve is 2.084 billion cu m, ranking first in China.

Most of Tibet's forest resources are concentrated in the southeastern part of the autonomous region, including the mountain areas of the Himalayas in the southern parts of Xigaze and Shannan prefectures, the Nyang River and Parlung Zangbo valleys in Nyingchi, and the Hengduan Mountains in Medog, Zayu and Qamdo Prefecture. The main forest types are sub-alpine dark conifers, such as a good variety of spruce and fir, with the commonly seen dominant species being Himalayan fir, Balfour spruce, purple-cone spruce, Lijiang spruce, hemlock and deciduous pines. There is also a wide distribution of alpine pine, Himalayan pine, Huashan pine and other needle-leaf trees in the Hengduan Mountains, and there are also China savin, alpine oak and other drought-resistant varieties in some valleys. Central Asian longleaf pine and Himalayan spruce are found in the Gyirong area in the central-western section of the Himalayas.

The spruce and fir forests in Tibet are mostly in a primitive state, with about four-fifths of them being mature or over-mature. They are highly productive biologically. Generally, one ha has over 500 cu m of timber in reserve, and even as high as 2,400 cu m per ha in some places, such as Bomi in Nyingchi. Some individual types of trees have 60 cu m in reserve each, which is a rare degree of productivity. The trees are straight and hard, so they are important building materials. The second-most important forests in Tibet are alpine pines, which have 130-150 cu m in reserve per ha. They are suitable for planting on barren land or as firewood on the plateau, because they can stand drought and poor soil, and grow rapidly, usually taking 20 to 30 years to grow to their full height.

In addition, there are tropical monsoon forests and subtropical evergreen broadleaf forests in the low mountainous and hilly lands in the Great Canyon of the Yarlung Zangbo and on the southern slope of the Himalayas. They total two million ha, with an estimated reserve of 400 million cu m.

Although forests cover only 10 percent of the total land area of the Tibet Autonomous Region, lower than the national average of 14 percent, their absolute amount, however, is large, so they are one of the region's major biological resources and a valuable asset for the plateau. Moreover, they are a natural ecological barrier protecting the natural environment of the plateau and producing important ecological benefits.

3. Farmland

At present, the total acreage of farmland is stable at about 230,000 ha, about two percent of Tibet's total land area. It is mainly concentrated in the valleys along the middle reaches of the Yarlung Zangbo and its tributaries, the Lhasa River, the Nyangqu River, Nyang River, and others, as well as some wide valley floors along the Jinsha, Lancang and Nujiang rivers in eastern Tibet. The area of "one river plus two tributaries" along the middle reaches of the Yarlung Zangbo boasts 176,000 ha of farmland, accounting for more than half of Tibet's total.

Most farmland in Tibet is suitable for growing *qingke* barley, wheat, rape, peas and other crops which thrive in cool climates, with one crop harvested a year. In the valleys of the "three rivers" in southern Qamdo, where the climate is relatively warm, farmland is scattered but is also suitable for growing corn, in addition to *qingke* barley, wheat and rape, with three crops reaped within two years or two crops reaped a year.

There are close to 2,000 ha of rice paddies in the low, warm valleys in Medog and Zayu, which are the only rice-producing areas in Tibet.

Due to climatic and terrain factors, the Tibetan plateau has little room for the expansion of farmland. The best way to improve cultivation is to raise per-ha output.

4. Flora

There are 6,800 higher plants in Tibet, and 39 wild plants among them are listed as major nationally protected wild plants, such as common reevesia, which is a first-class nationally protected plant, and big cypress, which is a second-class nationally protected plant, as well as Forrest Douglas fir, meranti, naked flower tetrameles, red toona, tetracentron and China yew.

Species of medicinal herbs number more than 1,000, of which 400 are commonly used in traditional Tibetan medicine, such as Chinese caterpillar fungus, bulb of fritillary, rose-boot, alpine rhubarb, gastrodia, milkvetch, thorowax, incised notopterygium, Tengshen (pilose Asiabell), large-leaf gentian, glossy ganoderma, *fuling* (poris cocos) and snow lotus.

The forest areas in eastern Tibet are famous for their tasty edible fungi, such as pine mushrooms, hedgehog hydnum, morels, scaly tooth and dried mushrooms, as well as common types of fungi.

There are 110 varieties of edible oil-bearing plants, notably smooth pit peach and oil fruit.

There are more than 70 species of aromatic plants for use in essences, perfumes and medicine, such as mint, elsholtzia, Thomson spicebush and sage.

The varieties of fibrous plants for weaving cloth, sacks and ropes number more than 100, such as moxanettle, water ramie, *bajiao* banana, winter daphne, ghost-arrow peashrub and white rattanpalm.

Starchy plants include alpine oak, Himalayan filbert, farges oatchestnut, fernhemp cinquefoil, and various varieties of the common yam.

Sugary plants suitable for brewing and making jam are plants of the rose family, blackberries, sandthorns and sugar palms.

Natural and artificially bred garden plants include winter jasmine, azalea, China flowering crabapple, winter daphne, rough gentian, rose, snow lotus and meconopsis. Most of them are alpine plants.

5. Fauna

Tibet boasts 799 vertebrate species, of which birds number 488, accounting for 40 percent of the national total bird species. Twenty-two species are unique to Tibet. There are 142 types of mammals, accounting for 32 percent of the national total; 56 types of reptiles, accounting for 28 percent of the national total; 45 types of amphibians, accounting for 22 percent of the national total; and 68 types of fish, of which schizothorocic carp makes up more than 90 percent of the world total in terms of numbers and variety.

Some 125 types of wild animals are listed as under state protection, accounting for more than one third of the total number of varieties under state protection. Forty-five of them are found only on the Qinghai-Tibet Plateau, such as Tibetan wild ass, wild yak, Tibetan antelope, ibex, snow leopard, black-necked crane and bearded vulture, which are species under first-class state protection. In the Himalaya and Hengduan mountains are found Assamese macaques, Yunnan golden monkeys, white-browed, long-armed gibbons, pigtailed monkeys, sun bears, Neofelis nebulosa (cloud-like spotted leopard), Bengal tigers, white-lipped deer, Przewalski's gazelles, takins, Himalayan tahrs, Ciconia boyciana, golden eagles, Tetrastes sewerzowi, crimson-bellied tragopans, Chinese monals and boa constrictors, which are all also species under first-class state protection.

Some wild animals can provide fine-quality meat, skin and plumes, while most of the others, especially those listed under state protection, are valued for use in medicine and scientific research as well as for cultural exchanges with other countries. Eighteen nature reserves at the national and regional levels have been established in Tibet in order to effectively protect the biological diversity of the plateau and ensure the utilization of biological resources in a sustainable manner and a benign circle of the natural ecology.

6. Hydropower

The Tibetan plateau is home to some well-known rivers in East Asia — the Yarlung Zangbo-Brahmaputra, Nujiang-Salween, Lancang-Mekong, and Jinsha-Yangtze. It is also where the upper streams of the Indus and other rivers originate or flow through. In addition, there are more than 1,000 lakes of various sizes and modern glaciers with a total area of roughly 27,400 sq km.

Tibet is rich in water resources, with average annual total water resources of 448.2 billion cu m, accounting for about 16 percent of the national total and ranking first among all the provinces and autonomous regions in China. The average annual total water resources of the Yarlung Zangbo alone are 165.4 billion cu m, more than one-third of Tibet's total. The modern glaciers in Tibet have an equivalent of 4,282 cu km of water, roughly amounting to 75 times the total volume (57.45 billion cu m) of the water the Yellow River empties into the sea every year.

The rivers in Tibet have a tremendous hydropower potential. Preliminary statistics put the average natural hydropower potential at 200,000 mw, accounting for about 30 percent of the national total and ranking first in China. The potential generating capacity of the utilizable hydropower is roughly 56,590 mw, with an annual power output of 330 billion kwh, or 17.1 percent of the national total. The per-capita exploitable hydropower resources are nearly 60 times the national average.

7. Geothermal Energy

Situated on the Himalayan section of the global geothermal band, Tibet has extensive zones of strong hydrothermal-type geothermal manifestations, topping the country in geothermal resource reserves. So far, 660 locations of various hydrothermal activity manifestations have been discovered, including hydrothermal explosions, geysers, boiling springs, hot springs, steaming zones and sinters. According to initial surveys conducted by the Chinese Academy of Sciences on 330 spots, the total volume of hot spring water is 20,000 liters per second and the total thermal energy is 660 mw per second, an energy equivalent of approximately three million tons of standard coal a year. Tibet's annual hydroelectric power potential exceeds 800 mw.

The Yambajain Geothermal Field at Damxung at the foot of the Nyainqentanglha Mountains is the largest field of geothermal manifestation discovered so far in Tibet. The temperature of the geothermal water in the shallow strata is 170 degrees centigrade, and 261.3 degrees centigrade at a depth of 2,000 m, the highest temperature of any such water in China. The total annual quantity of heat released equals the burning of 480,000 tons of standard coal, with a power-generating potential of 179 mw. The geothermal electric power station built there, the largest of its kind so far in China, has an installed generating capacity of 25 mw and a designed output of 130,000 mwh. It is now one of the main power suppliers to Lhasa City. Therefore, Lhasa's seemingly inexhaustible geothermal resources will become one of the major sources of new energy, with bright prospects for development.

8. Solar Energy

Tibet has the richest solar energy resources in China. In northern Tibet, which is the heartland of the plateau, the total annual solar radiation amount is as high as 5,900-7,400 mj per sq m. In the valleys along the middle reaches of the Yarlung Zangbo, the figure is 5,000-8,000 mj per sq m, and the total hours of sunshine are 2,000-3,300 per annum, with the sunshine percentage reaching 75 percent.

The country's highest total annual solar radiation amount has been recorded in the area surrounding the Rongpu Monastery at the foot of the Himalayas, 5,000 m above sea level, which is 8,370 mj per sq m.

The rich solar energy source can compensate for the plateau's insufficiency in temperature and thermal level. It not only greatly helps the growth of field crops and forests of economic value and orchards, but also, as a renewable energy, it can play a big role in developing greenhouse cultivation and industry related to environmental protection such as solar water heaters, and in the reduction of fossil fuel consumption and pollution from waste water, waste gas and waste materials.

9. Mineral Deposits

Tibet enjoys extremely favorable conditions for mineralization as it is situated at the eastern end of the Alps-Himalayas mineralization belt, one of the world's largest such belts. Initial prospecting has so far discovered four large-scale mineralization areas — eastern Tibet, the Himalayas, Gangdise and Changtang.

Ninety-four kinds of minerals have been discovered in Tibet. Among the dominant minerals are copper, chrome iron and lake salt. Tibet ranks second in China after Jiangxi Province in prospective copper reserves. The porphyry-copper deposit in Yulong, Jomda County, in eastern Tibet has a reserve of more than six million tons, which is rare in China and even in the world. So far, four porphyry-copper deposits have been discovered in eastern Tibet in association with more than ten other metals — lead, zinc, gold, silver, platinum, nickel, molybdenum, cobalt, tungsten and iron. Quite a few of them are up to or surpass the national standards for classifying large-scale mineral deposits and give Tibet a competitive edge.

Tibet has the richest chrome iron reserves in China, which have been found within an area of 2,500 sq km. The chrome iron content exceeds 50 percent. According to initial prospecting, the chrome iron deposit at Luobasha, in southern Tibet, amounts to more than four million tons, accounting for more than 85 percent of Tibet's total reserves and being the country's largest deposit of the mineral. Mount Qamka and Kangjinla in the vicinity of Luobasha also have sizeable reserves.

Tibet is an area with the largest number and the most complete range of salt lakes in the world. It has 250 salt lakes of various types, with a total area of

8,000 sq km and 140 million tons of reserves.

Among the non-metallic deposits, the verified reserve of magnesite, an auxiliary material in iron smelting, ranks third in the country; the reserves of barite and arsenic, which are urgently needed in the chemical industry, rank third and fourth in the country, respectively; and the reserves of gypsum and pottery clay, widely used in the building materials industry, rank second and fifth in the country, respectively. The verified peat reserve is more than 8 million tons, ranking fourth in the country, with the peat reserve in Jidaguo, Damxung, reaching 5.1 million tons. A number of oil and gas deposits have been discovered in Changtang and Lunpola in northern Tibet. Other major deposits include the Wuqimazala coalfield, with a reserve of 1.7 million tons, the Bungna Zangbo alluvial gold deposit, with a reserve of 10.1 tons, in Xainza, in northern Tibet, as well as another 113 areas showing evidence of gold, and deposits of diatomaceous earth, Iceland spar, corundum, crystal and agate.

图书在版编目（CIP）数据

西藏自然资源与自然风光 /李明森 杨逸畴 著.
－北京：外文出版社，2003.12
（西藏基本情况丛书）
ISBN 978-7-119-03454-6
Ⅰ.西... Ⅱ.①李...②杨... Ⅲ.自然地理－概况－西藏－英文
Ⅳ.P942.75
中国版本图书馆CIP数据核字（2003）第090578号

英文翻译： 王宗引
英文审定： 李振国
摄 影： 杨逸畴 李明森 张词祖 和桂华 杜泽泉
奚志农 卯晓岚 金志国 邵小川
责任编辑： 蔡莉莉
装帧设计： 蔡 荣
印刷监制： 冯 浩

西藏自然资源与自然风光

李明森 杨逸畴 著

©2010外文出版社
出版发行：
外文出版社（中国北京西城区百万庄大街24号）
邮政编码：100037
网址：http://www.flp.com.cn
电话：008610-68320579（总编室）
008610-68995852（发行部）
008610-68327750（版权部）
制版：
外文出版社照排中心
印刷：
北京京都六环印刷厂
开本：880mm×1230mm 1/32
2005年第1版第1次印刷 2010年第1版第2次印刷
（英）
ISBN 978-7-119-03454-6
06200（平）
17-E-3588 P